Book S

"ATMOSPHERE CHANGERS" is available to ANYONE who desires to learn kingdom weapons of demonic destruction that shifts atmospheres and establishes the kingdom of God in the earth realm.

As we move into a new dispensation within the Body of Christ, God desires to plant His kingdom in the earth realm as never before. His desires is not only that we praise and worship Him, but that we use our kingdom weaponry to shift and plant the attributes of heaven into the earth realm, while establishing the kingdom of heaven in our households, lineages, churches, communities, and regions; thus becoming kingdom shifters and atmosphere changers, within our sphere of influence. God is releasing unique weapons and there strategic usage in this season to assists us with establishing the victory and promises that are already manifested for us within the kingdom of heaven.

Since God is a spirit, He is going to use spiritual methods to bring His plans to pass. Even when He is utilizing natural means He is using spiritual instruments. We see this when Jesus walked the earth clothed in flesh. He was a spiritual being with a spiritual plan. As we embrace this fact about God, we can thus embrace that though God's weaponry may not make much natural sense, they are making perfect sense in the spirit realm and they possess the power to manifest God's spiritual knowledge and desires into our natural lives. This book explores various kingdom weaponry that pull down strongholds and principalities, while establishing and activating God's kingdom in the earth realm.

Atmosphere Changers

TaquettaBaker@Kingdomshifters.com

(Website) Kingdomshifters.com

Connect with Taquetta via Facebook or Youtube

Copyright 2011 – Kingdom Shifters Ministries

Taquetta's Bio

Taquetta Baker is the founder of Kingdom Shifters Ministries (KSM). She has authored fourteen books and two decree CD's. Taquetta has a Master's Degree in Community Counseling with an emphasis on Marriage, Children and Family Counseling, a Bachelor's Degree in Psychology and Associates Degree in Business Administration. In addition, Taquetta has a Therapon Belief Therapist Certification from Therapon Institute and has 22 years of professional and Christian Counseling experience.

Taquetta is also gifted at empowering and assisting people with launching ministries, businesses and books and provides mentoring, counseling and vision casting through Kingdom Shifters Kingdom Wellness Program. Taquetta serves on the Board of Directors for New Day Community Ministries, Inc. of Muncie, IN. In October 2008, Taquetta graduated from the Eagles Dance Institute under Dr. Pamela Hardy and received her license in the area of liturgical dance. Before launching into her own ministry, Taquetta served at her previous church for 12 years. She was a prophet, pioneer and leader of Shekinah Expressions Dance Ministry, teacher, member of the presbytery board, and overseer of the Altar Workers Ministry. Taquetta receives mentoring and ministry covering from Bishop Jackie Green, Founder of JGM-National PrayerLife Institute (Phoenix, AZ), and was ordained as an Apostle on June 7, 2014.

Taquetta flows through the wells of warfare and worship and mantles an apostolic mandate of judging and establishing God's kingdom in people, ministries, communities, and regions. Taquetta travels in foreign missions and throughout the United States. She has mentored and established dance, altar workers, deliverance, and prophetic ministries. Taquetta ministers in the areas of fine arts, all manners of prayer, fivefold ministry, deliverance, healing, miracles, atmospheric worship, and empowers and train people in their destiny and life's vision.

Connect with Taquetta and KSM at kingdomshifters.com or via Facebook. For more information regarding Bishop Jackie Green at Jgmenternational.org.

Table of Contents

KINGDOM SHIFTERS' CHARGE!
Heaven Invade Our Earth!

We command the earth realm to become agitated by the Holy Power of God. Kingdom Ambassadors, Appointed Leaders, God's Chosen Brides of Christ! Receive the fruit, the pleasures and fullness of the kingdom! Heaven demonstrate that we serve Jesus, the only true living God! Darkness must fall flat...Satan's imps and plans!!! It's your fate to bow!!!!

We decree a shift in the womb of our church, the body of Christ, our lineages and lifestyles and prophecy that divine mobility, recognizable change…A new season of contending has availed....miracles are forming...and invading; We ignite a merging of heaven in earth...even in tribulation, we establish that more are with us and ours than with them, therefore, ALL IS WELL!!!.

Stagnation Go!!! Spiritual paralysis be no more!!! Cycles and evil patterns we sever you from our sphere of influence while sounding an alarm that death has been defeated…Abundant life and destiny unlock as we thrust forcibly through your doors.

Heaven cause a deep penetration of our kingdom availability. Poignant piercings rain strategically

1

crushing, annihilating, discombobulating....dismantling our enemies. The battle is the Lord's yet we receive the victories. Jesus loose angels to war, bless, overcome, and deliver on our behalf, as we accelerate from level to level...maneuvering bountifully from glory to glory.

We speak clearly to the third heavens and contend for a synchronization of the throne of our King and our earth. Godly mantles fall with revelation of who we are in You; kingdom heirs ruling in dominion over the creepy and offensive....Ambassadors settling for nothing less than a pursuit for righteousness and our covenant worth.

Worshipping children enjoying God from their youth! Generations obediently walking in spirit and in truth...Equipping and sending forth with a global mandate; Prophecies fulfilled as God's word breeds, produce and reproduce...His will, His fruit!!!

We declare "Come Get Your Glory Lord!" For unrelenting praise and worship honorably awaits you! Empower and execute; establish and decorate; make our earth and sphere of influence Your very throne room! Overwhelm its' very existence establishing that

Your kingdom reigns. Once Your heaven invades our earth, eternity shifts into our present day!

WE CHARGE YOU LORD TO INVADE OUR EARTH!
ATMOSPHERE CHANGERS' CHARGE!
Atmosphere Changers Invade Earth With Heaven!

You were called and chosen to release the Kingdom of Heaven upon the earth just like Jesus did! YOU, my dear brother and sister in Christ, are the vehicle through which heaven and earth align and God's kingdom becomes manifest in the earth realm. Living your life from the reality of heaven towards the Earth should be your daily experience.

I assure you, most solemnly I tell you, if anyone steadfastly believes in Me, he will himself be able to do the things that I do; and he will do even greater things than these, because I go to the Father. (John 14:12)

God has called you to invade the Earth with His presence and given you the power of Heaven. Because you carry the Life of Jesus within you, the kingdom of heaven is at hand whereever you go.

And as you go, preach, saying, The kingdom of heaven is at hand! Cure the sick, raise the dead, cleanse the lepers, drive out demons. Freely (without pay) you have received, freely (without charge) give. (Matt 10:7-8)

4

The Spirit of God flows through you so that you CAN heal the sick when needed, you CAN give out the word of God to people that launches them into their destiny, and you CAN release the abundant life of Christ into every situation you encounter.

He who believes in Me [who cleaves to and trusts in and relies on Me] as the Scripture has said, From his innermost being shall flow [continuously] springs and rivers of living water. (John 7:38)

You are called in Christ to be Atmosphere Changers. A people who change the atmosphere by bringing the kingdom of heaven down to earth, wherever they are, wherever they go- Just like Jesus did and because of what Jesus did!

If you live in Me [abide vitally united to Me] and My words remain in you and continue to live in your hearts, ask whatever you will, and it shall be done for you (John15:17)

It's time for Heaven to Invade the Earth. So…what are you waiting for?

CHARGE!!!

In Him
Mignon Murrell
Rua Ministries

5

KINGDOM WEAPONRY

As we move into a new dispensation within the body of Christ, God desires to plant His Kingdom in the earth realm as never before. His desire is not only that we praise and worship Him, but that we use our kingdom weaponry to shift and plant the attributes of heaven into the earth realm, while establishing the kingdom of heaven in our households, lineages, churches, communities, and regions; thus becoming kingdom shifters, atmosphere changers, within our sphere of influence. God has and is releasing unique weapons and there strategic usage in this season to assists us with establishing the victory and promises that are already manifested for us within the kingdom of heaven.

2Corinthians 10:4-6 declares the following:

KJV

For the weapons of our warfare are not carnal, but mighty through God to the pulling down of strong holds; Casting down imaginations, and every high thing that exalteth itself against the knowledge of God, and bringing into captivity every thought to the obedience of Christ.

Amplified

For the weapons of our warfare are not physical [weapons of flesh and blood], but they are mighty before God for the overthrow and destruction of strongholds, [Inasmuch as we] refute arguments and theories and reasonings and every proud

6

and lofty thing that sets itself up against the [true] knowledge of God; and we lead every thought and purpose away captive into the obedience of Christ (the Messiah, the Anointed One).

The Message
The world is unprincipled. It's dog-eat-dog out there! The world doesn't fight fair. But we don't live or fight our battles that way – never have and never will. The tools of our trade aren't for marketing or manipulation, but they are for demolishing that entire massively corrupt culture. We use our powerful God-tools for smashing warped philosophies, tearing down barriers erected against the truth of God, fitting every loose thought and emotion and impulse into the structure of life shaped by Christ. Our tools are ready at hand for clearing the ground of every obstruction and building lives of obedience into maturity.

Weapon in this scripture is *Haplon* and means:

1. any tool or implement for preparing a thing
2. arms used in warfare, weapons
3. an instrument

Sometimes we negate the weapons and strategies, the instruments that God gives because we don't understand them. In our natural minds it is difficult to grasp how love casts out fear. We question praise and its ability to override the spirit of heaviness. We don"t grasp fully forgiving our adversaries and releasing them into the hands of

7

the Lord for Him to avenge. I am learning time and time again, that it is essential to be okay that God"s ways aren"t carnal or fleshy. I am learning to be at peace with the fact that His ways aren't my ways and the importance of taking hold of this concept, and aligning with Him even when I don"t fully comprehend all that His ways entails. God has and is releasing unique weapons in this season to assists us with establishing the victory and promises that are already available to us in the kingdom of heaven.

Since God is a spirit, He is going to use spiritual methods to bring His plans to pass. Even when He is utilizing natural means He is using spiritual instruments. We see this when Jesus walked the earth clothed in flesh. He was a spiritual being with a spiritual plan. As we embrace this fact about God, we can thus embrace that though God's weaponry may not make much natural sense, they are making perfect sense in the spirit realm and they possess the power to manifest God"s spiritual knowledge and desires into our natural lives.

Luke 10:17-20 reads:

> *(Amplified)*
> *The seventy returned with joy, saying, Lord, even the demons are subject to us in Your name! And He said to them, I saw Satan falling like a lightning [flash] from heaven. Behold! I have given you authority and power to trample upon serpents and scorpions, and [physical and mental strength and ability] over all the power that the enemy [possesses]; and nothing shall in any way harm you. Nevertheless, do not rejoice*

at this, that the spirits are subject to you, but rejoice that your names are enrolled in heaven.

(Message)
The seventy came back triumphant. "Master, even the demons danced to your tune!" Jesus said, "I know. I saw Satan fall, a bolt of lightning out of the sky. See what I've given you? Safe passage as you walk on snakes and scorpions, and protection from every assault of the enemy. No one can put a hand on you. All the same, the great triumph is not in your authority over evil, but in God's authority over you and presence with you. Not what you do for God but what God does for you--that's the agenda for rejoicing."

When Jesus said He saw Satan fall like lightening, this was an act that occurred in the spirit realm that yielded proof that His name was conquering in the earth realm. Jesus went on to tell the disciples not to rejoice that they can cast out devils but rejoice that the agenda of God is established for them and others as they do the work of the Lord. That agenda was that they were restored into the kingdom of heaven and were now partakers of God's heavenly attributes. This is what God's spiritual weapons achieve for us. They aren't carnal deeds, but spiritual accomplishments that further align earth with the plan and purposes of heaven.

Another facet we can contend from this passage of scripture is that as we are going forth as ambassadors for Christ, spiritual victories are

occurring within the spirit. As the disciples cast out demons in Jesus name, Jesus saw the defeat of Satan in the spirit realm. As we are used as ministering agents for God, there are spiritual victories occurring that is establishing God"s judgment in the earth. Satan was being brought down to the feet of Jesus as the disciples delivered people in Jesus name. Just as Jesus, we must have a greater awareness of what our natural actions are doing in the spirit realm and even what the purpose is for what we are manifesting.
Otherwise, we will have a joyful time being used of the Lord as the disciples did, but our ministry will lack the full understanding that as we deliver souls from the enemy, God's original plan and intent for our lives is being established among us.

KINGDOM DISCERNMENT

Discernment is essential to shifting and changing atmospheres so that God's kingdom can reign in our midst.

<u>Discernment in the Greek is *Diakrisis* and means:</u>
1. judicial
2. estimation
3. discern
4. disputation

<u>The primitive root word for *Discernment* is *Diakrino* and means:</u>
1. to separate, make a distinction, discriminate, to prefer
2. to learn by discrimination, to try, decide
3. to determine, give judgment, decide a dispute
4. to withdraw from one, desert
5. to separate one's self in a hostile spirit, to oppose, strive with dispute, contend
6. to be at variance with one's self, hesitate, doubt

<u>Hebrews 5:14 states:</u>
> *(KJV)*
> *But strong meat belongeth to them that are of full age, [even] those who by reason of use have their senses exercised to discern both good and evil.*

(Amplified)
But solid food is for full-grown men, for those whose senses and mental faculties are trained by practice to discriminate and distinguish between what is morally good and noble and what is evil and contrary either to divine or human law.

Discernment is what allows us to distinguish what is good and what is evil and to detect the blockages, strongholds, etc. that are hindering the presence and will of God from prevailing and triumphing in our lives and spheres of influence.

Ephesians 6:12 asserts:

(KJV)
For we wrestle not against flesh and blood, but against principalities, against powers, against the rulers of the darkness of this world, against spiritual wickedness in high [places].

There are countless teachings on the demonic kingdom. I will therefore only give a personal brief description of the hierarchies in Ephesians 6:12 as a basis for what will be discussed in this book.

- o **Principalities** are satanic princes and territorial spirits ruling over a nation, city, region, and community for the purposes of establishing Satan's demonic plan in people lives and spheres.
- o **Powers** are high ranking supernatural demons or demonic influences that cause evil and sin in the world.

- Rulers of Darkness are demonic forces that govern deception and manipulative hardships and catastrophes that are generally produced by witchcraft, manipulation of the weather and worldly systems; they operate in cultures and countries such that idolatry and sin rein in the earth.
- Spiritual Wickedness in High Places are evil plots and deceptions, and demonic attacks directed in and against the church and God's people for the purposes of hindering, contaminating and demolishing God's will in the earth.
- Strongholds are demonic possess or depression; demonic grip, harassment, influences, or hindrance that prevents a person from being free to walk in the full salvation for the Lord.

I am the leader of a dance ministry called Shekinah Expressions. The anointing and mandate of our dance ministry is to shift atmospheres and open spiritual airways so that the glory of God can reign. We use dance movements, drama and creative expressions to combat principalities and sever demonic strongholds via intercession, warfare, and praise and worship. The key is intentionality and understanding that we are not just dancers but ambassadors of Christ with specific callings to open the heavens, to establish the kingdom of Heaven in our midst, and to execute God's judgment in the earth realm.

Within our services, we minister in dance during praise and worship. The Lord will have us minister as a unified front and we use movements and various expressions and weapons of the Lord to combat any obstacle blocking the airways and preventing God's will from manifesting. There are instances where we will minister warfare moves, other times we will stand on a scripture, decree, prophetic word or promise, while manifesting God's purpose through movement. The Lord may have us march around the church or clap and release strike blows against the enemy. We may act out what the Lord gives us by displaying a spontaneous skit that demonstrates God's desires to deliver and set people free. At times, we will minister warfare or celebration movements that release judgment against or victory over the enemy. We recognize which weapons to utilize, by first discerning what we are combating or ministering and then seeking God for a strategy to take our rightful place of victory over it.

When searching out the spirit realm, one must be able to discern:
- when the heavens are open and it's a time to rest, celebrate, worship, decree, and reap the pleasures that are inside the presence of the Lord
- when the heavens are closed and need to be open so that God can work

- when principalities or territorial spirits are preventing the heavens from being opened
- when religion, tradition, and man's plans are hindering God from working and establishing His judgment
- when the people are bound by strongholds and/or worldliness and intercession is needed to release them to a place of liberty, salvation, healing and deliverance in God

There are instances where God may not necessarily speak His desires verbally. This is where it is essential for us as God's initial weaponry, to know how to discern His language, presence and to have relationship with Him so we can tap into the kingdom mysteries that He said would be given unto us as we mature in spiritual knowledge and understanding.

Matthew 13:11-17 Jesus states:

(Amplified)
And He replied to them, to you it has been given to know the secrets and mysteries of the kingdom of heaven, but to them it has not been given. For whoever has [spiritual knowledge], to him will more be given and he will be furnished richly so that he will have abundance; but from him who has not, even what he has will be taken away.

This is the reason that I speak to them in parables: because having the power of seeing, they do not see; and having the power of hearing, they do not hear, nor do they grasp and

15

*understand. In them indeed is the process of
fulfillment of the prophecy of Isaiah, which says:
You shall indeed hear and hear but never grasp
and understand; and you shall indeed look and
look but never see and perceive.
For this nation's heart has grown gross (fat and
dull), and their ears heavy and difficult of
hearing, and their eyes they have tightly closed,
lest they see and perceive with their eyes, and
hear and comprehend the sense with their ears,
and grasp and understand with their heart, and
turn and I should heal them.*

*But blessed (happy, fortunate, and to be envied)
are your eyes because they do see, and your ears
because they do hear. Truly I tell you, many
prophets and righteous men [men who were
upright and in right standing with God] yearned
to see what you see, and did not see it, and to
hear what you hear, and did not hear it.*

Mysteries in the Hebrew is Mysterion and means:

1. hidden thing, secret, mystery
2. generally mysteries, religious secrets, confided
    only to the initiated and not to ordinary mortals
3. a hidden or secret thing, not obvious to the
    understanding
4. a hidden purpose or counsel
5. secret will, of men, of God: the secret counsels
    which govern God in dealing with the
    righteous, which are hidden from ungodly and
    wicked men but plain to the godly

Jesus was saying that we have the spiritual ability to discern the spiritual intent of people, situations, climates, atmospheres, etc. Because we have accepted Him as Lord and are ministers of His glory, we possess the capacity to hear and see things that those who aren't of Him can't see, hear, or comprehend.

God speaks in various ways and so sharpening our discernment, our spiritual sight and hearing is key to knowing what He is speaking and displaying to us while pursuing strategy to further birth His desires and kingdom in our midst. Thus God may also reveal such mysteries through:

- Visions and mental pictures or movie type stories or projections
- Heart and soul burdens: Sometimes, God will place His burden in our heart or soul that provides information about what He is feeling and/or desires
- Physical sensations or impressions: Sometimes a person may feel within the spirit realm or within their body what is occurring in the atmosphere of the church, a community, city, state, nation, heavenlies, or in the people. For example, if a church is bond by religion, I may spirit a strong spirit of suffocation or death and even start to cough because my breathing is being cut off. I don't have a cold and I am not naturally

choking, but spiritually, I am experiencing the suffocation that is taking place within the atmosphere of that church.

- Emotional sensations or impressions: Though God is a Spirit; He has emotions and feelings just like we do and uses our emotions and feelings to speak to us. Sometimes a person will experience a strong emotion that is not theirs. For example, there are times when I will enter a city and if there is heavy oppression or poverty I will feel depressed. I won't be depressed but am picking up what is going on in the spirit realm of that city.

Often times, what happens within the body of Christ is that some will move out of familiarity without discerning and seeking God for the mysteries and strategies so that He can release His weapon necessary for raining victory. We will keep toiling with no real direction or purpose, or we will end services without the fullness of God's will manifesting. Sometimes, we will sit years in a church with a closed heaven, ignorant to the fact that there is sooooooo much more God desires us to have and experience in Him. It is important that our spiritual senses are enlightened so we can detect the enemy from the Lord, and be able to discern how to manifest our kingdom inheritance.

Paul states the following in Ephesians 1:17-23:

(Amplified)

[For I always pray to] the God of our Lord Jesus Christ, the Father of glory, that He may grant you a spirit of wisdom and revelation [of insight into mysteries and secrets] in the [deep and intimate] knowledge of Him, by having the eyes of your heart flooded with light, so that you can know and understand the hope to which He has called you, and how rich is His glorious inheritance in the saints (His set-apart ones).

And [so that you can know and understand] what is the immeasurable and unlimited and surpassing greatness of His power in and for us who believe, as demonstrated in the working of His mighty strength, which He exerted in Christ when He raised Him from the dead and seated Him at His [own] right hand in the heavenly [places], far above all rule and authority and power and dominion and every name that is named [above every title that can be conferred], not only in this age and in this world, but also in the age and the world which are to come.

And He has put all things under His feet and has appointed Him the universal and supreme Head of the church [a headship exercised throughout the church], Which is His body, the fullness of Him Who fills all in all [for in that body lives the full measure of Him Who makes everything complete, and Who fills everything everywhere with Himself].

The word *Knowledge* in the Hebrew is *Epignosis* and means:

1. precise and correct knowledge
2. used in the New Testament of the knowledge of things ethical and divine

The primitive root word of *Knowledge* is *Epiginosko* and means:

1. to become thoroughly acquainted with, to know thoroughly
2. to know accurately, know well
3. to know
4. to recognize
5. by sight, hearing, of certain signs, to perceive who a person is
6. to know i.e. to perceive
7. to know i.e. to find out, ascertain
8. to know i.e. to understand

The most effective way to sharpen our discernment and enlighten our spiritual knowledge of His Word will, and ways, is to spend time with God and learn His presence. In His presence, we are able to build a relationship by partaking of Him, feasting off His goodness, and tasting and sensing His ways, His will, and His desires.

Psalms 34:8 declares:

> *(KJV)*
> *O taste and see that the LORD is good: blessed is the man that trusteth in him.*

(The Message)
Open your mouth and taste, open your eyes and see — how good GOD is. Blessed are you who run to him.

Webster's dictionary defines *Taste* as:

1. to try or test the flavor or quality of (something) by taking some into the mouth: to taste food
2. to eat or drink
3. to perceive or distinguish the flavor of:
4. to have or get experience, especially a slight experience
5. to perceive in any way, to enjoy or appreciate, examine by touch; feel, to test or try
6. to try the flavor or quality of something, to smack or savor
7. the sense by which the flavor or savor of things is perceived when they are brought into contact with the tongue
8. to relish, liking, or partiality for something
9. the sense of what is fitting, harmonious, or beautiful; the perception and enjoyment of what constitutes excellence in the fine arts, literature, fashion, etc.
10. one's personal attitude or reaction toward an aesthetic phenomenon or social situation, regarded as either good or bad
11. the ideas of aesthetic excellence or of aesthetically valid forms prevailing in a culture or personal to an individual

It is in His presence that we revealed knowledge of His goodness and partake of Him. This sets the stage for distinguishing His will, from our soulish desires, the enemies" tactics and the world's ways. I learned from my mentor an essential key of beginning my prayer time is by cleansing my eye gates, ear gates, sense of smell, touch, taste, atmosphere and imagination with the blood Jesus. I apply Jesus blood to purge any contamination of self, the world, TV, people, religion, the demonic etc., so that when I am in the presence God, I will have a purer experience of encountering Him and being able to discern Him from the enemy, self, the devil, etc. This is vital as an atmosphere changer, because it helps one quickly discern and expose darkness and pursue God further for strategic weapons to dispel it.

There are times where God may not outright speak on a matter and you aren't sure what you are discerning but just know it isn't the Lord. This can happen in ministry and in everyday life. When this occurs, I generally ask the Holy Spirit to lead my endeavors and I wait till He is totally in charge. Then as I am totally submitted, I follow His leading in exposing and dismantling the culprit. During these instances where Shekinah Expressions is ministering during praise and worship, the Holy Spirit has led us to stand on a scripture while ministering in dance. We would pick a scripture that gives us power over the enemy or something of that nature and keep battering with it until the blockage is removed. The enemy hates unity so there have been

22

instances where we will all join hands or lock arms and just stand in position or minister movements in unison. Though we will discuss this more in the praise and worship section, unison, is a weapon within itself and breaks the back of the enemy because he is one of discord and confusion.

Psalms 144:1 says:
>*(KJV)*
>*He teaches my hands to war and my fingers to fight.*

This book provides different weapons for shifting spheres and establishing the kingdom of heaven. However, it is God that teaches us to war and how to fight so we can win the war. Therefore, after you discern the hindrances to God's will in a particular situation, for the weaponry and strategy needed for bringing His kingdom in your midst. He may lead you to one in this book or a unique one. I love when God release unique weapons as it shows that He isn't limited to this world or our reasoning. He is always out the box and working outside the box. Don't limit Him and you will be surprised what He reveals to tower the enemy. Let's move forward to exploring weaponry.

WEAPONRY OF PRAISE & WORSHIP

Praise and worship is the greatest corporate weapon we have within the kingdom of God. I always tell people if you don't worship and praise God, you will worship and praise something. I believe praise and worship are innate and is one of the essential functions of our existence.

In Deuteronomy 6:4-5, God command the Israelites:
> *(Amplified)*
> *Hear, O Israel: the Lord our God is one Lord [the only Lord]. And you shall love the Lord your God with all your [mind and] heart and with your entire being and with all your might.*

God adamantly commands the Israelites to love Him, the only Lord, with everything within them. He knew that what they loved, they would celebrate and worship and He knew the risk and consequences of exalting and worshipping anything less or above Himself.

Praise and worship in and of itself is apostolic in nature because when expressed with abandonment, it releases power to shift atmospheres and establish judgment in the earth realm. And depending on who and what you are praising and worshipping, determines the culture created and the judgment released.

All through the Bible and even today, we see the consequences of praising and worshipping idols. Many miss out on the promises of God, His will and destiny for their lives and heaven altogether. The challenge with praising and worshipping idols is one reaps the demonic casualties of the enemy while inheriting the wrath and judgment of God.

Exodus 20:2-6 declares:
(Amplified)
I am the Lord your God, Who has brought you out of the land of Egypt, out of the house of bondage. You shall have no other gods before or besides Me. You shall not make yourself any graven image [to worship it] or any likeness of anything that is in the heavens above, or that is in the earth beneath, or that is in the water under the earth; You shall not bow down yourself to
them or serve them; for I the Lord your God am a jealous God, visiting the iniquity of the fathers upon the children to the third and fourth generation of those who hate Me, but showing mercy and steadfast love to a thousand generations of those who love Me and keep My commandments.

This alone should behoove us to praise and worship no other god while recognizing the love and merciful benefits of praising and worshipping the only true and living God.

The word says that God inhabits the praises of His people.

Psalms 22:3 reveals:

(KJV)
But thou art holy, O thou that inhabitest the praises of Israel.

(The Message)
And you! Are you indifferent, above it all, leaning back on the cushions of Israel's praise?

And not only does God inhabit our praises; He comes bearing gifts of joy and pleasures beyond our imagination.

Psalms 16:11 affirms:

(KJV)
Thou wilt shew me the path of life: in thy presence is fulness of joy; at thy right hand there are pleasures for evermore.

When God inhabits our praises, He comes to reveal the path and plan for our lives. He comes to bring pleasures that break chains of bondage and sets us free to walk in the original plans and intents to which He created us. He comes in response to our love for Him and as we praise and worship Him, He in turn, bestows His love upon us.

We definitely can encounter God and the heavenlies when we praise and worship during our personal prayer time, but there is even great power when we enter corporate praise and worship. Praise and worship then becomes an even greater weapon that can discombobulate and dismantle the enemy and establish God's judgment in the earth realm.

Matthew 18:19-20 states:

> *(KJV)*
>
> *Again I say unto you, that if two of you shall agree on earth as touching anything that they shall ask, it shall be done for them of my Father which is in heaven. For where two or three are gathered together in my name, there am I in the midst of them.*

We see the fruit of this scripture in *2 Chronicles 20 (Amplified)*, when the Moabites, the Ammonites, and the Meunites declared war against Jehoshaphat and Judah. Jehoshaphat set a fast and gathered Judah into the assembly to seek God for a word and strategy.

> *Verse 3- 4*
>
> *Then Jehoshaphat feared, and set himself [determinedly, as his vital need] to seek the Lord; he proclaimed a fast in all Judah. And Judah gathered together to ask help from the Lord; even out of all the cities of Judah they came to seek the Lord [yearning for Him with all their desire].*

Jehoshaphat stood before all of Judah and declared God's greatness and all He had done within the ancestral line of the Israelites. He expressed to the Lord in *verse 7-9*:

> *Did not You, O our God, drive out the inhabitants of this land before Your people Israel and give it forever to the descendants of Abraham Your*

friend? They dwelt in it and have built You a
sanctuary in it for Your Name, saying, If evil comes
upon us, the sword of judgment, or pestilence, or
famine, we will stand before this house and before You-
-for Your Name [and the symbol of Your presence] is in
this house--and cry to You in our affliction, and You
will hear and save.

Jehoshaphat knew from experience that dwelling
in the midst of God's presence, drew His
deliverance and saving power, while establishing
God's judgment over every demonic infestation
and judgment of the enemy. For we see in verse
12, that He inquires to whether God will release
His judgment and deliver them as He has in times
past.

> *O our God, will You not exercise judgment upon*
> *them? For we have no might to stand against*
> *this great company that is coming against us.*
> *We do not know what to do, but our eyes are*
> *upon You.*

God then releases this word and promise of
deliverance to Jehoshaphat and all of Judah:

> *Verse 11-19*
> *Then the Spirit of the Lord came upon Jahaziel*
> *son of Zechariah, the son of Benaiah, the son of*
> *Jeiel, the son of Mattaniah, a Levite of the sons of*
> *Asaph, in the midst of the assembly. He said,*
> *Hearken, all Judah, you inhabitants of Jerusalem,*
> *and you King Jehoshaphat. The Lord says this to*
> *you: Be not afraid or dismayed at this great*
> *multitude; for the battle is not yours, but God's.*
> *Tomorrow go down to them. Behold, they will*
> *come up by the Ascent of Ziz, and you will find*

*them at the end of the ravine before the
Wilderness of Jeruel.*

*You shall not need to fight in this battle; take
your positions, stand still, and see the
deliverance of the Lord [Who is] with you, O
Judah and Jerusalem. Fear not nor be dismayed.
Tomorrow go out against them, for the Lord is
with you.*

Jehoshaphat and Judah responded by worshipping
and praising the Lord, simply on the bases of His
word.

Verse 18-19
*And Jehoshaphat bowed his head with his face to
the ground, and all Judah and the inhabitants of
Jerusalem fell down before the Lord, worshiping
Him. And some Levites of the Kohathites and
Korahites stood up to praise the Lord, the God of
Israel, with a very loud voice.*

In the next chapter we are going to explore the
power that praise has to execute judgment. Yet I
do want to note that when the Levites of
Kohathites and Korahites stood up to praise, God,
they did so in a very loud voice.

The word *Loud* in the scripture is *Gadowl* and
means:

1. great
2. large (in magnitude and extent), in number
3. in intensity
4. loud (in sound)

5. older (in age)
6. in importance
7. important things
8. great, distinguished (of men)
9. God Himself (of God)

When they praised loudly, they went forth with intensity, in great number (corporately), and with a strategic focus to give God abandoned praise. Yet more importantly we see that one of the definitions of *loud* is, "God Himself (of God)." WHEEEEEWWW! When they praised, they were releasing the very voice of God, which shifted the atmosphere to one of faith and belief in standing on the word God had just given them.

And on next day, when they went forth against their enemies with faith in the word, and praised and worshiped further, there corporate praise and worship, established the word God has spoken to them within their midst, such that there enemies turned on one another…killing themselves.

> *Verse 20-22*
> *And they rose early in the morning and went out into the Wilderness of Tekoa; and as they went out, Jehoshaphat stood and said, Hear me, O Judah, and you inhabitants of Jerusalem! Believe in the Lord your God and you shall be established; believe and remain steadfast to His prophets and you shall prosper. When he had consulted with the people, he appointed singers to sing to the Lord and praise Him in their holy*

[priestly] garments as they went out before the army, saying, Give thanks to the Lord, for His mercy and loving-kindness endure forever!

And when they began to sing and to praise, the Lord set ambushments against the men of Ammon, Moab, and Mount Seir who had come against Judah, and they were [self-] slaughtered; For [suspecting betrayal] the men of Ammon and Moab rose against those of Mount Seir, utterly destroying them. And when they had made an end of the men of Seir, they all helped to destroy one another.

HIGH PRAISE THAT EXECUTES JUDGEMENT

Psalms 149 declares:
> *(Amplified)*
> *Praise the Lord! Sing to the Lord a new song,*
> *praise Him in the assembly of His saints! Let*
> *Israel rejoice in Him, their Maker; let Zion's*
> *children triumph and be joyful in their King!*
> *Let them praise His name in chorus and choir*
> *and with the [single or group] dance; let them*
> *sing praises to Him with the tambourine and*
> *lyre! For the Lord takes pleasure in His people;*
> *He will beautify the humble with salvation and*
> *adorn the wretched with victory. Let the saints*
> *be joyful in the glory and beauty [which God*
> *confers upon them]; let them sing for joy upon*
> *their beds. Let the high praises of God be in their*
> *throats and a two-edged sword in their hands, to*
> *wreak vengeance upon the nations and*
> *chastisement upon the peoples, to bind their*
> *kings with chains, and their nobles with fetters*
> *of iron, to execute upon them the judgment*
> *written. He [the Lord] is the honor of all His*
> *saints. Praise the Lord! (Hallelujah!)*

Psalms 149 begins with the commandment to
Praise the Lord! That word *"praise"* is *Halah* in the
Hebrew and is the same word used for *"praise"* in
2Chronicles 20.

Praise in that scripture is *Halah* and means:

1. to shine

2. to shine (fig. of God's favour)

3. to flash forth light
4. to praise, boast, be boastful
5. boastful ones, boasters (participle)
6. to praise
7. to boast, make a boast, glory, make one's boast
8. to be praised, be made praiseworthy, be commended, be worthy of praise
9. to make a fool of, make into a fool
10. to act madly, act like a madman

Such praise requires complete abandonment of self in boldly declaring the due adoration of the Lord. But not just to declare it, to boast His greatness while being so caught up in exalting Him, that the very praise itself jails the enemy, assault his land, and executes the judgments and plans of the Lord among people and nations.

We discern this as we read the mandate of verses 6-9:

> Let the high praises of God be in their throats and a two-edged sword in their hands, to wreak vengeance upon the nations and chastisement upon the peoples, to bind their kings with chains, and their nobles with fetters of iron, to execute upon them the judgment written. He [the Lord], is the honor of all His saints. Praise the Lord! Hallelujah!

In many churches today we have praise and worship going forth, and we are even experiencing the presence of God, but rarely is there a display of praise and worship that execute vengeance upon God's enemy and establish His will within the region of that church or community, less known nation. We have great musicians and singers. Great choirs and praise and worship teams and have even added dancers and flaggers and on and on. We have a presentation of tabernacle worship and are even seeing miracles and healings at times. We experience transformation at times and because we have touched God and felt Him, we assumed we have reached our mandate to praise and worship Him until His dominion has been made known with clarity and precision. But what we are truly experiencing is a lot of works and giftings in operation that is producing an effect of Christ...an effect of heaven and His kingdom, but the truly calling of our mandate and giftings are not in operation nor manifesting complete Godly results. Our actions are not fully exercised such that a true constant result of Psalms 149 is manifesting and creating continual kingdom results that brings eternity into our earth realm. We have furthermore, used ridiculous religious excuses of the reasons this isn't so. Even to the point of marking revivals and displaying temporary moves of God as if God extinguishes His own mandate to show forth signs and wonders and even offering other excuses to justify why we see temporary effects of the kingdom rather than a full vengeance and judgment of God's working being done in our efforts of what we contend is true praise and worship.

Praise in Psalm 149 states *to shine, to boast, to act like a mad man*...wildly before God. It admonishes us to sing and praise with all that is within us unto the Lord. Such an expression isn't about how we feel, dependent on whether God answers our prayers, based on how we look to others, whether God responds to our actions or any of the other man made excuses or insecurities we use to determine how much of ourselves we offer up to God. It isn't based on what we think we will lose or gain but really is about grasping an understanding that our praise and worship speaks forth the oracles of God, gives Him voice in our midst, and provides an avenue for Him to establish His Lordship as savior and King of the whole earth, in the entire universe.

I have heard some of the greatest singers speak about holding back during praise and worship for fear of losing their voice. I have seen some of the most talented dancers operate out of insecurity and shame and not give fully over to their giftings because of the faces of the people. Saints sit down on God Service after service, refusing to praise Him, bow before Him and be liberated in their expression of love for Him. They are more concerned about how they look or the murmurings and mockery of the people than exemplifying a true reverent fear of the Lord. No, everyone will not jump pews or run around the church. But true praise and worship is a complete abandonment of the heart, mind, and soul such that when you have totally engaged God, a piece of Him has changed some facet of your life. If you do not experience a shift or transformation via praise and worship then

35

you have not fully tapped into the vein…true vine of God where His kingdom judgments can be established in your life. For true praise and worship intercedes for you. It produces for you. It literally and physically manifests among you who you are declaring God to be. And even if you may not immediately see it in the natural realm, if you truly gave undo admonishment, you will sense that change and transformation has occurred in the natural.

Do not just take my word for it but let's explore Psalm 149 further. Verses 6-9 state:

> Let the high praises of God be in their throats and a two-edged sword in their hands, to wreak vengeance upon the nations and chastisement upon the peoples, to bind their kings with chains, and their nobles with fetters of iron, to execute upon them the judgment written. He [the Lord] is the honor of all His saints. Praise the Lord! (Hallelujah!)

A high praise sets off an alarm while declaring the judgment of God.

High in the Hebrew is _Rowmĕmah_ and means:
1. Uplifting
2. Arising

The primitive root word of *High* is *Ruwa* and means:

1. shout, noise, alarm
2. cry, cry out
3. triumph
4. raise a sound
5. give a blast
6. to shout a war-cry or alarm of battle
7. to sound a signal for war or march
8. to shout in triumph (over enemies)
9. to shout in applause
10. to shout (with religious impulse)
11. to cry out in distress
12. to utter a shout, a shout for joy
13. to shout in triumph
14. to shout for
15. destroyed

Ruwa is also same Hebrew word for the word *"Shout"* mentioned in Joshua 6 when the Israelites sought to possess the promise land.

Joshua 6:1-5
(KJV)
Now Jericho was straitly shut up because of the children of Israel: none went out, and none came in. And the LORD said unto Joshua, See, I have given into thine hand Jericho, and the king thereof, and the mighty men of valour. And ye shall compass the city, all ye men of war, and go round about the city once. Thus shalt thou do six days. And seven priests shall bear before the ark seven trumpets of rams' horns: and the seventh day ye shall compass the city seven times, and the priests shall blow with the trumpets. And it shall come to pass, that when they make a long blast with the ram's horn, and when ye hear the sound of the trumpet, all the people shall shout

with a great shout; and the wall of the city shall
fall down flat, and the people shall ascend up
every man straight before him.

When the Israelites shouted, they were releasing a
high praise that declared the Lord's judgment
regarding victory over Jericho. Despite Jericho
being under siege and unable to go in and out of
the city, they didn't even recognize that a war was
already in effect. They recognized the armed
Israelites and saw the marching but they didn't
realize that the marching, silence, and eventually
sounding of the trumpets were actually war. They
didn't comprehend that the Israelites were already
engaging them in war through this strategic plan
that was provided by God. They were waiting for
a battle to take place that had actually already
broken out in the spirit realm.

In Jos 6:16, Joshua tells the people to shout for God
had given them the city.

> *And it came to pass at the seventh time, when*
> *the priests blew with the trumpets, Joshua said*
> *unto the people, Shout; for the LORD hath given*
> *you the city.*

Jericho was a gateway to where the Israelites were
going. It also was a stronghold because there was
no way to get to the promise land except the
Israelites pass through Jericho. So, Jericho was the
city that was standing between what God had said
was theirs.

The shout the Israelites released was one of victory for what had already taken place in the spirit realm and was about to materialize in the natural realm. So, when the people shouted, the wall fell down flat; the materialization of the spiritual work manifested and the Israelites took the city. We see this in verse 20 of Joshua 6:

> *So the people shouted when [the priests] blew with the trumpets: and it came to pass, when the people heard the sound of the trumpet, and the people shouted with a great shout, that the wall fell down flat, so that the people went up into the city, every man straight before him, and they took the city.*

Imagine your roof blowing off your home. Should this happen, your home is subject to rain, strong wind, bird droppings, bugs and God only knows what else. You are unprotected and can"t resist whatever takes flight over you. Jericho was exposed on all sides and therefore had basically fallen to the hands of the Israelites without even engaging in battle. When the walls fell, it exposed the enemy and made it impossible for the city of Jericho to resist the Israelites. It wreaked God's vengeance upon Jericho and chastisement upon the people.

The walls represented a territorial principality, as no one could get through to the other parts of the land, without going through Jericho. But when the Israelites shouted, it bound the demonic kings and nobles over Jericho and brought down the territorial principality. It demolished the principality and activated the generational word that was already written concerning the Israelites. And that was that they would inherit the promise land.

Shouting can signify that a battle is taking place, about to take place, or has already taken place. It can also be a sign of victory, distress, or a signal to alarm those around you that we are in a place of battle or even distress, depending on the situation. *Psalms 47:5* says *God has gone up with a shout.* Basically this means God responds to shouting. His presence acts as a mediator when He hears His people shouting and most importantly, when He hears high praises going forth on His behalf.   The high praises signals Him to inhabit our cries and fulfill His word that if we praise Him in total abandonment, He will execute vengeance upon the enemy and establish His desires for us in the earth realm.

In 1Samuel 4, the word came to Samuel for Israel to battle against the Philistines. The elders of Israel decided to fetch the ark of the covenant of the Lord so they could have His presence in battle with them in effort to defeat the Philistines. Now, when the ark was being brought up from Shiloh where it was housed, the Israelites began to shout with a great shout that filled the earth (my God). The Philistines heard the noise of the shout and immediately recognized that the presence of God was with the Israelites and that they were in trouble. They became afraid as they themselves

40

said in verse 7, *"God is come into the camp. Woe unto us!"* Now, the Philistines won this war but only because Eli's sons had defiled the house of the Lord and Eli restrained them not (I Samuel 3). And as a result, God used the Philistines to judge the house of Eli. The Philistines did not win the battle because they were greater; they won because God allowed the defeat due to the sin being allowed in the temple of God.

Take a moment and imagine the victory that would have taken place if Eli's sons and the Israelites in general, were in order with God. The Philistines already felt defeated from discerning the shout of Israel. With the shout alone they knew God's presence was with the Israelites and they were about to be slaughtered. They recognized they had messed with the wrong people and no good could come of it. If Israel's shout could exude this and they were in defiance to God, imagine what your shout says to your enemies when you are in order with God? Imagine the trembling that takes place in the spirit realm when you alarm the devil with your high praise that God is on your side.

High praises aren't so much about pitch as it is about depth and precision of what you are spewing. I can yell Jesus inside my mind and sound just as much of an alarm as if I yelled His name verbally. The key is what my alarm is, who I'm triggering, and whether I am aware of the power and stance to which my alarm stems from. Often we are yelling and making noise but many do not have revelation for the purposes of praise or

41

the purposes of praising Jesus. So our sounds trigger nothing spiritually and thus lack the effect of birthing the fruit of the kingdom. And even though it isn't about volume, at times, volume is necessary to wreak vengeance upon the enemy. We laugh at the loud folks in the church and even talk negative about them. Yet their actions are biblical and necessary to casting fear and dread upon the enemy. As atmosphere changes we must yield high praise to draw God into fulfilling His word that if we praise, He will come to deliver His kingdom into our earth realm.

SONGS THAT SHIFT
ATMOSPHERES

Ephesians 5:17-20 contends:

(KJV)
Wherefore be ye not unwise, but understanding what the will of the Lord is.

And be not drunk with wine, wherein is excess; but be filled with the Spirit; Speaking to yourselves in psalms and hymns and spiritual songs, singing and making melody in your heart to the Lord; Giving thanks always for all things unto God and the Father in the name of our Lord Jesus Christ;

(The Message)
Don't live carelessly, unthinkingly. Make sure you understand what the Master wants. Don't drink too much wine. That cheapens your life. Drink the Spirit of God, huge draughts of him. Sing hymns instead of drinking songs! Sing songs from your heart to Christ. Sing praises over everything, any excuse for a song to God the Father in the name of our Master, Jesus Christ.

As a person who was a heavy drinker before being saved, I find it very interesting that Paul would consider being filled with the Holy Spirit a substitute for drinking. And then to express further that we are to esteem ourselves with spiritual songs while keeping a constant attitude of thanksgiving unto the Lord. Yet, looking back, often when I became intoxicated, I would find

43

myself singing what the Message Bible calls "drinking songs," to the top of my lungs. They didn't sound very good and I'm sure though pretty hilarious, were at times, humiliating.

Paul is saying by being intoxicated with the Holy Spirit, we can have that same level of joy and even greater without degrading ourselves and cheapening who we are in God. One thing we know about a drunk, they can either be the life of the party or can ruin a party. Depending on how the alcohol affects their mood, a drunk can either yield great pleasure to everyone around them or wreak much havoc and turmoil. Yet to the Lord, a drunk outside of the Spirit is one of debauchery.

Colossians 3:16-17 affirms:

(KJV)
And whatsoever ye do in word or deed, do all in the name of the Lord Jesus, giving thanks to God and the Father by him. Let the word of Christ dwell in you richly in all wisdom; teaching and admonishing one another in psalms and hymns and spiritual songs, singing with grace in your hearts to the Lord. And whatsoever ye do in word or deed, do all in the name of the Lord Jesus, giving thanks to God and the Father by him.

(The Message)
And cultivate thankfulness. Let the Word of Christ – the Message – have the run of the house. Give it plenty of room in your lives.

Instruct and direct one another using good common sense. And sing, sing your hearts out to God! Let every detail in your lives – words, actions, whatever – be done in the name of the Master, Jesus, thanking God the Father every step of the way.

How does singing shift atmospheres? From these scriptures alone, we can conclude that the most efficient attributes that singing ushers in is joy and thanksgiving unto the Lord. It is difficult to be depressed, fearful, negative, double-minded, confused, etc., when one is making melody unto the Lord.

Isaiah 61:1-3 declares:

(KJV)
*The Spirit of the Lord GOD [is] upon me; because the LORD hath anointed me to preach good tidings unto the meek; he hath sent me to bind up the brokenhearted, to proclaim liberty to the captives, and the opening of the prison to [them that are] bound; To proclaim the acceptable year of the LORD, and the day of vengeance of our God; to comfort all that mourn; To appoint unto them that mourn in Zion, to give unto them beauty for ashes, the oil of joy for mourning, **the garment of praise for the spirit of heaviness**; that they might be called trees of righteousness, the planting of the LORD, that he might be glorified.*

Praise in that passage of scripture is _Tehillah_ and means:

1. praise, song or hymn of praise
2. praise, adoration, thanksgiving (paid to God)
3. act of general or public praise
4. praise-song (as title)
5. praise (demanded by qualities or deeds or attributes of God)
6. renown, fame, glory
7. object of praise, possessor of renown

In this passage of scriptures, we see that the garment of praise is given in exchange for heaviness. Praise in this instance refers to songs and hymns of adoration and thanksgiving unto the Lord. Isaiah 61 begins by stating, _"The Spirit of the Lord God is upon me."_

The Hebrew word for _Spirit_ is _Ruwach_ and means:

1. wind, breath, mind, spirit
2. of heaven, breath of air, heaven
3. spirit (as that which breathes quickly in animation or agitation)
4. spirit, animation, vivacity, vigour, courage
5. prophetic spirit, as inspiring ecstatic state of prophecy
6. as gift, preserved by God, God's spirit, departing at death, disembodied being
7. spirit (as seat of emotion), desire, as seat or organ of mental acts,

46

8. rarely of the will, as seat especially of moral character

9. Spirit of God, the third person of the triune God, the Holy Spirit, coequal, coeternal with the Father and the Son

10. imparting warlike energy and executive and administrative power

11. as endowing men with various gifts, as energy of life

12. as manifest in the Shekinah glory

The primitive root word for *Spiritual* found in Ephesians 5:19 is *Pneuma* and has the same meaning as the Hebrew word *Ruwach*. Both scriptures are referring to God's Holy Spirit.

The Hebrew and Greek definition of Spirit describes God's presence as His very breath or a wind. When a wind blows, a shift takes place. If it's a hot day and a cool breeze begins to blow, it cools off the day. Let's say you are at a picnic and all of a sudden, a hard wind comes rushing in. That hard wind will brisk through the trees, knocking down and blowing away everything that isn't nailed or tied down; as long as things didn't get destroyed or blow too far away, you may be able to recover them, and put them back into place. Nature's wind, just like a drunk, changes the atmosphere, WHEWWWWWWWWW!!! God's wind, His *Ruwach* wind,
not only shifts the atmosphere and everything in it, but transforms it so that even if it is put back into

position, it is never the same.   And if something
was destroyed, it must have been necessary, and
God restores it such that what He releases through
His Spirit is better than the original.

Ephesians tells us to be full of the Spirit, *"To drink
of it."* The requires us to spend time asking the
Holy Spirit to come and breath on us, consume us,
quench our thirst. Sometimes throughout the day,
I will just ask the Holy Spirit to come and drench
me and wait in His presence. And then there are
instances throughout the week where I will just
spend time drinking of the Holy Spirit but back to
spiritual songs.

Ephesians 20:17-20 states:
> *(KJV)*
> *Wherefore be ye not unwise, but understanding
> what the will of the Lord is. And be not drunk
> with wine, wherein is excess; but be filled with
> the Spirit; Speaking to yourselves in psalms and
> hymns and spiritual songs, singing and making
> melody in your heart to the Lord; Giving thanks
> always for all things unto God and the Father in
> the name of our Lord Jesus Christ;*

Spiritual in the Hebrew is *Pneumatikos* and means:
1. relating to the human spirit, or rational soul, as
   part of the man which is akin to God and serves
   as his instrument or organ
2. that which possesses the nature of the rational
   soul

3. belonging to a spirit, or a being higher than man but inferior to God
4. belonging to the Divine Spirit
5. of God the Holy Spirit
6. one who is filled with and governed by the Spirit of God
7. pertaining to the wind or breath; windy, exposed to the wind, blowing

Pneuma is the primitive root word of *Spiritual*, which is the Hebrew word for "Holy Spirit." So Paul is admonishing us to sing songs, as when we do, we are birthing forth, spewing forth the *Pnuema* and *Ruwach* wind of God. Thus it shifts the atmosphere around us, while ushering in the presence and kingdom of God. And unlike natural wind, when we sing spiritual songs, Holy Spirit songs, chains of bondage are loosed and captives are set free. Spiritual songs draws souls to repentance, to receive Christ, and be water and spirit baptized. Such songs shift atmospheres and produce the will and desire of God so that His kingdom is established in the people, the culture, and the sphere around us. This is conveyed in Acts 16, when Paul and Silas were thrown in jail. Now before we get into Acts 16, I want to express that Paul was filled with the Spirit of God as this is what the word says in Acts 13:9,

> *Then Saul, (who also is called Paul,) filled with the Holy Ghost, set his eyes on him.*

Merriam Webster's Online Dictionary defines *Fill* as:

1. to make full; put as much as can be held into
2. to occupy to the full capacity
3. to supply to an extreme degree or plentifully
4. to satisfy fully the hunger of; satiate
5. to put into a receptacle
6. to be plentiful or extend throughout
7. to furnish with an occupant (WHEWWWWWW!!!)
8. to supply the requirements or contents of
9. to meet satisfactorily, as requirements
10. to stop up or close

JESUS!!!! In other words, Paul had spent time drinking the Holy Spirit, and seeming Silas accompanied him in ministry, we can assumed he had his life in order and was also a drinker of God's Spirit. In Acts 16, Paul and Silas were beaten and thrown in jail for delivering a sorcerer and preaching Jesus. Thus they were labeled as trouble makers. At midnight, Paul and Silas begin to pray and sing praises unto God and all the prisoners heard.

Acts 16:26-34 reads:
(KJV)
And at midnight Paul and Silas prayed, and sang praises unto God: and the prisoners heard them. And suddenly there was a great earthquake, so that the foundations of the prison

*were shaken: and immediately all the doors were
opened, and every one's bands were loosed.
And the keeper of the prison awaking out of his
sleep, and seeing the prison doors open, he drew
out his sword, and would have killed himself,
supposing that the prisoners had been fled. But
Paul cried with a loud voice, saying, Do thyself
no harm: for we are all here. Then he called for a
light, and sprang in, and came trembling, and
fell down before Paul and Silas, and brought
them out, and said, Sirs, what must I do to be
saved? And they said, Believe on the Lord Jesus
Christ, and thou shalt be saved, and thy house.
And they spake unto him the word of the Lord,
and to all that were in his house, and he took
them the same hour of the night, and washed
their stripes; and was baptized, he and all his,
straightway. And when he had brought them
into his house, he set meat before them, and
rejoiced, believing in God with all his house.*

Paul and Silas were so full of the Spirit of God, that
when they began to pray and sing, a great
earthquake manifested. Now that's what I call
mass weaponry that changes atmospheres! That's
some mighty kingdom shifting. The spiritual
songs that came out of them, caused an agitation, a
disruption, an upheaval, and sent fear and
trembling within the atmosphere of the jail. So
much so that the earthquake itself opened the door
and loosed the bands of the prisoners. The jail
keeper was so scared by what he had just
experienced, that he drew his sword to kill himself,
but Paul stopped him by yelling that everyone was
still in the prison even though they were no longer

bound (WHEWWWWW). The jail keeper was so amazed with the effects of Paul and Silas" praise and worship that he fell at their feet and sought salvation for him and his family. They shared the gospel of Jesus Christ with him, and he and his family gave their lives to Jesus and was baptized. The key to shifting atmospheres with spiritual songs is being filled, drinking and consuming the Spirit of God.

There are times during ministry where before or after our dance ministry ministers, the Lord will lead us to sing a spiritual song to further shift the atmosphere, and establish what He has sent us there to minister into the people, the climate or region. In the natural I cannot sing, so if you came to me and said sing "Jesus Loves Me" we would have a really good time laughing at how horrible I sounded. And I definitely do not profess to be a singer although I am always singing to Jesus. I am sure He just laughs because I laugh at myself. However, during some ministry engagements, the Holy Spirit will use our group to sing spiritual songs and often His presence has come in so magnificently, that it is difficult to move forward in the service. Often salvation, deliverance and healing will manifest and God will release a prophetic word or word of revelation to further save, encourage, or explain what He is doing. It is great to watch God's winds come in and take over a service. There is nothing like it, it will only increase one's desire to want more of Him, and more of His glory to be unveiled.

Spiritual songs are usually spontaneous in nature, are Holy Spirit inspired are sometimes, they are prophetic. They can also be a hook that is sung over and over as a means of battering an obstacle in the spirit realm until freedom takes place. I have also experienced people singing scriptures from the Bible. At any rate, spiritual songs are definitely an efficient weapon for seeing God's glory reign in the earth. Drink of Him and sing thanksgiving unto Him as much as possible. And watch Him shift you and your sphere from glory to glory in Him.

ATMOSPHERIC MUSIC

I first want to state the fact that atmospheric music prophesies and produces the spirit of prophecy:

1 Chronicles 25:1-3

> *(KJV)*
>
> *Moreover David and the captains of the host separated to the service of the sons of Asaph, and of Heman, and of Jeduthun, who should **prophesy** with harps, with psalteries, and with cymbals: and the number of the workmen according to their service was: Of Jeduthun: the sons of Jeduthun; Gedaliah, and Zeri, and Jeshaiah, Hashabiah, and Mattithiah, six, under the hands of their father Jeduthun, who prophesied with a harp, to give thanks and to praise the LORD.*

1 Samuel 10:5-7

> *(KJV)*
>
> *After that thou shalt come to the hill of God, where is the garrison of the Philistines: and it shall come to pass, when thou art come thither to the city, that thou shalt meet a company of prophets coming down from the high place with a psaltery, and a tabret, and a pipe, and a harp, before them; and they shall **prophesy**: And the Spirit of the LORD will come upon thee, and thou shalt **prophesy** with them, and shalt be turned into another man. And let it be, when these signs are come unto thee, that thou do as occasion serve thee; for God is with thee.*

I further want to contend that atmospheric music overrides evil so that the word of the Lord can come forth and dismantle the enemy and his plans. We see this in 2 Kings 3, we find King Moab rebelling against King Jehoram, ruler of Israel, by refusing to pay his annual tribute of 100,000 rams and sheep. King Jehoram was wicked and did evil in the site of the Lord but Jehoshaphat, King of Judah and King of Edom, joined him in war against King Moab out of respect for their ancestral heritage. But when they were in the route to war, they journeyed to an area that had no water for the animals or soldiers. King Jehoshaphat inquired, as to whether there was a prophet available that could give a word from the Lord, and Elisha was recommended because the word of the Lord was with him.

The three kings visited Elisha and first he refused to prophecy because King Jehoram was wicked and was the son of Ahab and Jezebel. He told him to go get his parents" prophets. Out of respect for King Jehoshaphat, Elisha however, agreed to inquire of the Lord and asked for a minstrel so he could enter the presence of the Lord. The scriptures read as followed:

2Kings 3:14-20:

> *(KJV)*
> *And Elisha said, As the LORD of hosts liveth, before whom I stand, surely, were it not that I regard the presence of Jehoshaphat the king of Judah, I would not look toward thee, nor see thee. But now bring me a minstrel. And it came to pass, when the minstrel played, that the hand of*

the LORD came upon him. And he said, Thus saith the LORD, Make this valley full of ditches.

For thus saith the LORD, Ye shall not see wind, neither shall ye see rain; yet that valley shall be filled with water, that ye may drink, both ye, and your cattle, and your beasts. And this is but a light thing in the sight of the LORD: he will deliver the Moabites also into your hand. And ye shall smite every fenced city, and every choice city, and shall fell every good tree, and stop all wells of water, and mar every good piece of land with stones. And it came to pass in the morning, when the meat offering was offered, that, behold, there came water by the way of Edom, and the country was filled with water.

Elisha was a known prophet who had a double portion of His predecessor,
Elijah's Spirit.

2Kings 2:9

(KJV)
And it came to pass, when they were gone over, that Elijah said unto Elisha, Ask what I shall do for thee, before I be taken away from thee. And Elisha said, I pray thee, let a double portion of thy spirit be upon me.

Elisha had given words of the Lord before without the assistance of a minstrel so it is indeed interesting that in this instance, he would ask for one to be present. As I consider this passage of scripture, what is very intriguing is that Elisha would not have even inquired of the Lord had not

56

King Jehoshaphat been present. King Jehoram was ruler of Israel at the time but he was the son of Ahab and Jezebel, and the bible says that though he didn't sin like them, He cleaved to various sins of Jeroboam that caused Israel to sin against God.

2 Kings 3:1-3

(KJV)

Now Jehoram the son of Ahab began to reign over Israel in Samaria the eighteenth year of Jehoshaphat king of Judah, and reigned twelve years. And he wrought evil in the sight of the LORD; but not like his father, and like his mother: for he put away the image of Baal that his father had made. Nevertheless he cleaved unto the sins of Jeroboam the son of Nebat, which made Israel to sin; he departed not therefrom.

Just to give you a little back ground, Jeroboam was very rebellious and vengeful. He was Solomon's right hand man at one time but then plotted to be king and was run into exile. He returned after Solomon's death and put up cult shines that centered on worshipping the golden calf that the Israelites had worshipped when they first were delivered from Egypt (1Kgs 11:30-38; 12:19, 25-33; 2 Kgs 17:21-23, 2Chr 10-13). Though King Jehoram wasn't as evil as his parents, we can conclude that he had generational strongholds and curses from them and he cleaved, which means he basically cohabitated with idolatry.

Elisha knew that God was a jealous God and hated idolatry. Verse 3 says that because of idolatry,

57

God's presence had departed from Israel. Elijah therefore, needed a minstrel to draw in the presence of God so that he could hear His word and will for Israel, despite them being in a place of rebellion. King Jehoshaphat;s presence also allowed Elisha to beckon God because he served God, so that yielded further revelation to Elisha that though God had departed from Israel, He still loved the people and His hand upon some of them as King Jehoshaphat was the king of Judah and Judah serve God.

I believe the when the minstrel begin to play, the music consumed the atmosphere and declared God's rule within the region, over Israel, and among Elisha and the kings. God honored Elisha's and the minstrel's worship, and His presence came upon Elisha so God's will was declared concerning the war at hand.

Minstrel in the Hebrew is _Nagan_ and means:
1. play, player
2. to play a stringed instrument
3. to play and strike strings

An essential key definition of _minstrel_ is '_strike._' We will talk about _strike_ more in depth in the "Power of the Clap Chapter," but for now I want to iterate a few points about striking.

Webster's Online Dictionary describes _Strike_ as:
1. to hit forcibly
2. to ignite (a match)

3. to impress
4. to cancel
5. to afflict or affect
6. to find, as gold or oil
7. to deal a blow
8. to make an attack
9. to stop work to compel an employer's agreement to workers' demands
10. to sound by percussion

When a minstrel plays, they are striking the enemies that are in the atmosphere forcibly, such that it ignites a war that truly the enemy cannot win. The strikes stop the work of the enemy. They also force everything within its sphere to comply with the dominion of God. Minstrels therefore, have the ability to exude the hand of the Lord into a place, such that His presence comes to speak forth a word, and to dispel darkness and the likes of the enemy. Because minstrels are atmospheric, I believe that the playing itself was a prophetic act of what the Lord had Elisha to declare concerning Israel winning the war.

2Kings 3:18-19 reads:

(KJV)
*And this is but a light thing in the sight of the LORD: he will deliver the Moabites also into your hand. And ye shall **smite** every fenced city, and every choice city, and shall fell every*

good tree, and stop all wells of water, and mar
every good piece of land with stones.

Smite also means to strike. Webster's Online
Dictionary defines it as the following:

1. to strike or hit hard, with or as with the hand, a
   stick or a weapon.
2. to deliver or deal
3. to strike down, injure or slay
4. to afflict or attack with deadly or disastrous
   effect
5. to affect mentally or morally with a sudden
   pang, fear or smitten with terror.

What God spoke through Elisha as the minstrel
played, was being established in the spirit realm
such that when the Moabites rose up to fight the
Israelites the next day, they were met with a
bloody sea and thought the Israelites had turned in
on themselves. But to their surprise, the Israelites
where very much alive, and the blood they saw
was a sign of their own demise that had already
taken place in the spirit realm as their principalities
and demonic forces in the spirit realm had been
struck down when the minstrel played disastrous
blows, smiting their demonic realm with the
dominion of God's kingdom.

> *Verse 20-27 (KJV)*
> *And when all the Moabites heard that the kings*
> *were come up to fight against them, they*
> *gathered all that were able to put on armour, and*
> *upward, and stood in the border. And they rose*

up early in the morning, and the sun shone upon the water, and the Moabites saw the water on the other side [as] red as blood: And they said, This [is] blood: the kings are surely slain, and they have smitten one another: now therefore, Moab, to the spoil.

And when they came to the camp of Israel, the Israelites rose up and smote the Moabites, so that they fled before them: but they went forward smiting the Moabites, even in [their] country. And they beat down the cities, and on every good piece of land cast every man his stone, and filled it; and they stopped all the wells of water, and felled all the good trees: only in Kirharaseth left they the stones thereof; howbeit the slingers went about [it], and smote it.

Speaking of the demonic realm and the power of minstrels against them, lets" consider the story of David playing the harp when Saul would be oppressed by an evil spirit. **1Samuel 16:15-23 contends:**

(KJV)

But the Spirit of the LORD departed from Saul, and an evil spirit from the LORD troubled him. And Saul's servants said unto him, Behold now, an evil spirit from God troubleth thee. Let our lord now command thy servants, which are before thee, to seek out a man, who is a cunning player on an harp: and it shall come to pass, when the evil spirit from God is upon thee, that he shall play with his hand, and thou shalt be well.

61

And Saul said unto his servants, provide me now a man that can play well, and bring him to me. Then answered one of the servants, and said, Behold, I have seen a son of Jesse the Bethlehemite, that is cunning in playing, and a mighty valiant man, and a man of war, and prudent in matters, and a comely person, and the LORD is with him. Wherefore Saul sent messengers unto Jesse, and said, send me David thy son, which is with the sheep. And Jesse took an ass laden with bread, and a bottle of wine, and a kid, and sent them by David his son unto Saul.

*And David came to Saul, and stood before him: and he loved him greatly; and he became his armourbearer. And Saul sent to Jesse, saying, Let David, I pray thee, stand before me; for he hath found favour in my sight. And it came to pass, when the evil spirit from God was upon Saul, **that David took an harp, and played with his hand: so Saul was refreshed, and was well, and the evil spirit departed from him.***

Often times, Saul would solicit David to play for him when he would become oppressed with an evil spirit. God sent the evil spirit to possess Saul as part of his rejection and judgment for his sin of disobedience, for choosing the people's ways over God's ways, and sparing the life of King Agag when God told him to kill the King and everyone attached to him (1Sam 14-15). Saul knew that if David played, the spirit would depart and in his words, *"he would be well."* Saul understood the power of music and the ability for the minstrel to usher in the healing and deliverance power of God. The word says that as David played, the Saul was made well and refreshed and the evil spirit departed from Him. The evil spirit didn't hang out or lay dormant inside him. It left. It broke camp. It was expelled.

What Elisha's minstrel and David possessed was the presence of the Lord.
This takes us back to the previous chapter where we explored drinking the Holy Spirit. When a minstrel is anointed by God, miracles, healings, deliverance, signs and wonders follows his or her ministry. Even if you don't play music, listening to anointed music or being in the presence of music can birth forth great deliverance and healing. When the minstrels possess God's favor and His presence, they are able to shift atmospheres, declare and impede war upon the enemy, and establish victory within people's lives and the atmosphere around them.

ATMOSPHERIC DANCE

The earliest mention of dance in the Old Testament occurred in Exodus 15:20, when Prophetess Miriam took her timbrel and lead the women in dance as a victory celebration after the children of Israel successfully crossed the Red Sea while Pharaoh and his army drowned. Prophetess Miriam was allowed to lead the dance because in the Hebrew culture, the nearest relative to the forerunner of the victory was chosen to lead the celebration dance when a battle was won (*Scripture Look At Dance, Apostle Pamela Hardy*). Richard A Murphy wrote an article in 1998 called "Worship In Dance," and suggested that Israel viewed dance as a prophetic gift because during Miriam's time, dance, music, and instruments were taught in the school of prophets. Although the Bible never records one prophecy of Miriam, she was known in biblical history as a prophetess and for leading the Israelites in this celebration of deliverance.

The primitive root word for *dance* is *"Machashabah"* which means:
1. thought,
2. device
3. plan, purpose
4. invention

The word is saying that dance acts as a thought, device, and an invention that administers a strategic plan or purpose. Though the dance

Miriam lead wasn't what we would exactly consider prophetic today, it was very strategic in nature and significantly shifted and impacted the atmosphere, the future of the people, and the climate much like prophetic dance today. At an even greater stretch, it could even be suggested then that this first law of dance that Prophetess Miriam lead was apostolic as it celebrated the defeat of a national military force of elite troops that truly was the drowning of a principality.

Exodus 15:20-21 affirms:
> *(KJV)*
> *And Miriam the prophetess, the sister of Aaron, took a timbrel in her hand; and all the women went out after her with timbrels and with dances. And Miriam answered them, Sing ye to the LORD, for he hath triumphed gloriously; the horse and his rider hath he thrown into the sea.*

Pharaoh had held the Israelites captive and refused to let them go. But God prevailed on their behalf and Pharaoh and his army drowned in the red sea (Exo 14). This great procession of triumph that Prophetess Miriam led included singing and the use of the timbrel; the timbrel is a kingdom weapon representative of striking, to beat, to smite or kill. So she actually was in spiritual warfare.

Timbrel is the same Hebrew root word as *Tabering* which means:
to beat the breast which can include forms of dance as spiritual warfare and intercession.

Though naturally Prophetess Miriam was leading a dance of celebration, perhaps in the spirit realm she was completing and solidifying within the supernatural what had already occurred in the natural realm. Though Israel wondered in the wilderness for forty years, their fate within the slavery of Egypt was over from that day. Had they grasped this revelation on the day of celebration, their stay in the wildness may not have been as long.

When I teach dance, I express that we are not performers and we are not just ushering in the presence of God or to be representatives of praise and worship. We are ministers of the presence of God and are on a specific assignment to shift atmospheres and execute God's judgment and kingdom in the earth. Prophetess Miriam was a prime example that dance is more than just celebrating and twirling before God. Dance and movement in general exudes a faith and a release that has the potential to gain ground and establish a working in the spirit realm that can't be done with just words alone. We see that in the promise God made Joshua in Joshua 1:3:

> *(KJV)*
> *Every place that the sole of your foot shall tread upon, that have I given unto you, as I said unto Moses.*

We also can examine that in Isaiah 52:7,

> *(KJV)*
> *How beautiful upon the mountains are the feet of him that bringeth good tidings, that publisheth peace; that bringeth good tidings of good, that publisheth salvation; that saith unto Zion, Thy God reigneth!*

As the atmosphere changes it is important to understand that we weren"t called to be stagnant. Our entire being can be used to speak and bring forth the oracles of God and as we dance we are publishing the goodness of heaven among the earth.

It is essential to note that God gets His grove on. Not only is dance innate within us, it is a part of the image of God. Even God, our Great Creator and King rejoice in song and praise.

Zephaniah 3:17 states:

> *(KJV)*
> *The LORD thy God in the midst of thee is mighty; he will save, he will rejoice over thee with joy; he will rest in his love, he will joy over thee with singing."*

> *(The Message)*
> *The LORD your God is with you. He is a hero who saves you. He happily rejoices over you, renews you with his love, and celebrates over you with shouts of joy."*

The word *Rejoice* in that passage of
scripture is *Giyl* and means, to spin
around with violent or sudden emotion

What a revelation to know that God is celebrating
over us. He is dancing, singing, shouting,
spinning, and jumping up and down. That just as
we offer up praises unto Him, He too dances over
us with thanksgiving and praise.

If you study the Hebrew words that describe
dance, rejoice, or fear in the Old Testament you
will discern that many of them speak of violent
intercessory dance. Dancing was not meant to be
the passive, rhythmic movements we have made it
today; it is to be total abandonment, violent
intercession, uncontrollable emotion and
expression unto God. We tend to label these types
of people as weird, beyond peculiar, but really
they are demonstrating the true heart for God for
abandoned praise and worship.

All throughout biblical history, we see dance as an
integral part of the religious culture. It is evident
that God desires to move with us and through us.
When God made the earth, the word said in
Genesis 1:2,

> *(KJV)*
> *The Spirit of God moved upon the face of the*
> *waters.*

It was as if God's spirit was sashaying around the
earth and His presence and voice was sculpting

creation and fulfilling that which was empty and hallow. When God made Adam and Eve, He blessed them, and said in Genesis 1:28,

(KJV)
Be fruitful, and multiply, and replenish the earth, and subdue it.

Subdue in the Hebrew is *Kabash* and means:

1. to subject, subdue, force, keep under, bring into bondage
2. to bring into bondage, make subservient
3. to be subdue, force, violate
4. to dominate, tread down

Such movement implies a combating type of maneuvering. The definition puts me in remembrance of Matthew 11:12,

(KJV)
And from the days of John the Baptist until now the kingdom of heaven suffereth violence, and the violent take it by force.

Though we assume that such warfare and intercession was entered in after sin, it appears that even before sin, our dominion over the earth required us to conquer it, not just with our position but with our actions as kings and queens of the world. Sometimes I feel this when I am dancing in warfare, intercession or abandonment before the Lord. I can feel things materializing and growing inside of me, in others, within the atmosphere, and

69

even within the spirit and earth realm that didn't exist until my movements began to tread within the supernatural. I can also feel myself subduing land and possessions for the kingdom, or taking back what the enemy has stolen from people, climates and atmospheres; and often the results of these works materialize in the earth realm. Dance in the church today is actually a fulfillment of prophecy as Jeremiah 31:13 declares,

> *(KJV)*
> *Then shall the virgin rejoice in the dance, both young men and old together: for I will turn their mourning into joy, and will comfort them, and make them rejoice from their sorrow."*

As we rejoice in the dance, God will use our movements to shift atmospheres while dispelling darkness and releasing the fullness of His joy, His comfort, His pleasures, within people and within our sphere.

MARCHING IN SILENCE

There are times in our spiritual walk when we really want to tell someone what we think of them or a situation. Especially, when our actions are justifiable; or there are benefits in it for us that we really need in order for change to occur in our lives. It is often in these instances that the Lord will unction us to be silent. And if we haven''t trained ourselves to be obedient to the word of the Lord, we end up aborting His promises by speaking before it is time. There are times in life and even in warfare or intercession, where silence is essential for combating the enemy. During these times, the Lord may direct us to add other prophetic acts to counteract the silence. In the case of the Israelites, possessing the promise land, it was them marching in silence that was the prophetic act.

<u>Joshua 6:1-5 reads:</u>
>   *(KJV)*
>   *Now Jericho was straitly shut up because of the children of Israel: none went out, and none came in. And the LORD said unto Joshua, See, I have given into thine hand Jericho, and the king thereof, and the mighty men of valour. And ye shall compass the city, all ye men of war, and go round about the city once. Thus shalt thou do six days. And seven priests shall bear before the ark seven trumpets of rams' horns: and the seventh day ye shall compass the city seven times, and the priests shall blow with the trumpets. And it shall come to pass, that when they make a long*

blast with the ram's horn, and when ye hear the sound of the trumpet, all the people shall shout with a great shout; and the wall of the city shall fall down flat, and the people shall ascend up every man straight before him.

Verse 10 (KJV)
And Joshua had commanded the people, saying, Ye shall not shout, nor make any noise with your voice, neither shall [any] word proceed out of your mouth, until the day I bid you shout; then shall ye shout.

The word *Compass* in the Hebrew is *Cabab* and means:

1. to turn, turn about or around or aside or back or towards, go about or around, surround, encircle
2. change, to change direction, to march or walk around, go partly around, circle about, skirt, make a round, make a circuit, go about to, surround, encompass
3. to turn oneself, close round, turn round, to be turned over to
4. to turn about, change, transform, to encompass, surround, to come about, assemble round
5. to enclose, envelop
6. to turn, cause to turn, turn back, reverse, bring over, turn into, bring round
7. to cause to go around, surround, encompass, to be turned, to surround

Say for example I'm in the sixth grade and a bully took my stuff. My first inkling would be to pump myself up and approach the bully and demand my stuff back. This tactic would most likely get me knocked upside the head. But let's say I approached the bully and I said nothing but just walked around him in silence then walked away. At first the bully may mock me and try to embarrass me in front onlookers, but after a few days he would be baffled and probably even question my sanity and whether it was a good idea to take my stuff. The bully would most likely return my stuff at some point than to risk any further weird actions from me.

Jericho had to be baffled by the Israelites marching around them in silence. I am sure they had thoughts of attacking first but didn't want to risk defeat. I am sure they had thoughts of running but because the Israelites had shut them up in the city, there was no way to escape. They were probably doing all they could to prepare for the striking of the Israelites. Yet because the tactics of the Israelites were unusual, despite preparation, they were caught off guard by the strategies God had given Joshua.

Silence baffles the enemy and creates curiosity that can torment the enemy with fear and dread. Imagine sitting at your desk at work and someone comes in your office without saying anything, walks around your desk and then walks out. The first day you would be curious and probably would blow off the experience, but after the second, third and definitely by the seventh day you would be beyond confused and inquiring

73

about what is going on. Even when we are conversing and someone suddenly becomes silent, we begin to wonder what they are thinking. Sometimes, God want us to be quiet, even when we know His plans, as doing so gives us further control over the victory He is unfolding, and weakens the hand of the enemy. Silence makes the enemy vulnerable to our intents and while He is toiling, God is working through us to bring His will to past.

In this passage of scripture, the Lord coupled marching with silence. It was a two-fold weapon that allowed the Israelites to speak and birth forth the plans of God with movement rather than the spoken word. Have you ever seen someone lip sing a song while they are dancing and you wished they would stop the lip singing and just dance? That is because the lip singing is taking away from you being able to focus on the movements as you are then drawn to their mouths rather than watching the expressions going forth in their bodies. If the Israelites would have marched around while chattering, the seriousness of the assignment at hand would have been lessened. It would have also taken away from the power and impact of what God was doing through them by marching as they were taking up territory in the spirit realm. The marching I believe weakened the walls. It slowly crumbled the walls of Jericho in the spirit realm so when the people shouted and the trumpets sounded, the walls just fell down. The marching had already taken up ground in the spirit which in turn, manifested in the natural on the seventh day; the day of completion. And the silence provided them with the avenue to be able to march without interference from the enemy as if they would have been talking, it would have drew the enemy into attacking before the appoint time as the work in the spirit realm would still be establish.

There is an abundance of prophetic work we can do in the spirit realm through marching. I believe marching is an expression that we are not bound, as one can"t march unless they are actually picking up their feet and moving in an upward motion. This symbolizes that we are climbing and moving forward with each motion. Marching is very strategic as it symbolizes rule and dominion, rank, government, and even order in the spirit and natural realm. Even when someone marches in a band during a parade, motorists are made to pull over to the side to give way to those participating. Marching yields a level of ground that wouldn't be given under ordinary circumstances. *Romans 16:20* declares,

> *(KJV)*
> *And the God of peace shall bruise Satan under your feet shortly. The grace of our Lord Jesus Christ be with you. Amen.*

This is a prophetic scripture that speaks of the fate of Satan; It also yields reference to the power of our feet. When God judges Satan, it will be through the bruising of our feet. Our feet will therefore have to be moving for bruising to occur. I believe when we marching there is a bruising that takes place and when the final blow hits, the breakthrough comes. As kingdom shifters, we must be willing to use our movement to encompass the enemy. Silence with that allows us to maneuver among the enemy without Him recognizing that we are a threat that is about to destroy his strongholds and possess the promise land in our lives and those we are praying for and ministering too. Let me share a few scriptures to provide further revelation of this theory.

> **Deu 11: 24** *Every place whereon the soles of your feet shall tread shall be yours: from the wilderness and Lebanon, from the river, the river Euphrates, even unto the uttermost sea shall your coast be.*

> **Deu 33:29** *Happy art thou, O Israel: who is like unto thee, O people saved by the LORD, the shield of thy help, and who is the sword of thy excellency! and thine enemies shall be found liars unto thee; and thou shalt tread upon their high places.*

> **Jos 1:3** *Every place that the sole of your foot shall tread upon, that have I given unto you, as I said unto Moses.*

> **Psa 91:13** *Thou shalt tread upon the lion and adder: the young lion and the dragon shalt thou trample under feet.*

> **Psa 108:13** *Through God we shall do valiantly: for he it is that shall tread down our enemies.*

Mal 4:3 *And ye shall tread down the wicked; for they shall be ashes under the soles of your feet in the day that I shall do this, saith the LORD of hosts.*

Luk 10:19 *Behold, I give unto you power to tread on serpents and scorpions, and over all the power of the enemy: and nothing shall by any means hurt you.*

These scriptures are an entire lesson independently, and are just a mere glimpse of the power and authority that is in our feet. Let's be open to use the weapons of marching and silence and even using them collectively for the advancement and establishment of the kingdom.

EXPLOSIVE POWER OF YOUR CLAP

Clapping is just not an expression of praise and worship. It is not just an expression of joy or rejoicing and giving due applause. It can also be used prophetically and in warfare combat the enemy. It is my prayer that after you have read this chapter, you will no longer patty cake God for you will never see clapping the same way. There is demon busting explosive power in your clap.

Psalms 144

(KJV)

Blessed be the LORD my strength, which teacheth my hands to war, and my fingers to fight:

Psalms 18:30-34

(KJV)

For by thee I have run through a troop; and by my God have I leaped over a wall. As for God, his way is perfect: It is God that girdeth me with strength, and maketh my way perfect. He maketh my feet like hinds' feet, and setteth me upon my high places. He teacheth my hands to war, so that a bow of steel is broken by mine arms.

When dancing before the Lord with one of my mentee, the Lord gave her a revelation that our hands are daggers and they can be spiritually and naturally detrimental or beneficial depending in how we use them. She expressed further that the Lord said that sometimes our hand movements are daggers and are being used to surgically cut

78

people open so that He could perform surgery on them, and other times they are used to destroy and conquer darkness. This revelation is confirmation of the above scriptures and how God teach our hands to war and our fingers to fight. Even as I consider this revelation further, God is giving me a vision of bright glowing swords being attached to my arms rather than hands and they are slicing through darkness, the camp of the enemy. But I am not in control for it is as if the Lord is maneuvering my hands and even though I can"t see what"s in the darkness, He is instructing my hands on how to move, which way to move, and what to pierce and cut.

Webster"s Online Dictionary defines *Dagger* as:

1. a short, sword like weapon with a pointed blade and hand, used for stabbing
2. to stab with or as if with a dagger, a switchblade
3. to mark with a dagger

God is the teacher of the dagger. He is the one who instructs our hands of His operations. And though we simply see hands, God sees swords, daggers that are used to shift people and atmospheres and administer judgment so that His victories can prevail among us.

THE EXPLOSIVE WARFARE CLAP

Psalms 47(KJV)

> O clap your hands, all ye people; shout unto God with the voice of triumph. For the LORD most high is terrible; he is a great King over all the earth. He shall subdue the people under us, and the nations under our feet. He shall choose our inheritance for us, the excellency of Jacob whom he loved. Selah. God is gone up with a shout, the LORD with the sound of a trumpet.

> Sing praises to God, sing praises: sing praises unto our King, sing praises. For God is the King of all the earth: sing ye praises with understanding. God reigneth over the heathen: God sitteth upon the throne of his holiness. The princes of the people are gathered together, even the people of the God of Abraham: for the shields of the earth belong unto God: he is greatly exalted.

In this scripture *Clap* in the Hebrew means *Taqa*

1. to blow, clap, strike, sound, thrust, give a blow, blast
2. to thrust, drive (of weapon)
3. to give a blast, give a blow
4. to strike or clap hands
5. to be blown, blast (of horn)
6. to strike or pledge oneself

This Psalms provide clear revelation concerning the power of the clap and that clapping can be a great weapon for atmospheric change. Here we see that though the clap is to exalt God, He more importantly, is using the clapping of the hands to assert His authority among nations and to establish the inheritance of His people. He is encouraging the people to clap and shout so that His blows of war can go forth through them while being administered into the atmosphere of the nation around them. And as they clap and shout He lets them know that He has been exalted even more and Has sounded an alarm against the enemy:

> *Verse 7 (KJV)*
> *God is gone up with a shout, the LORD with the sound of a trumpet.*

Often when the praise and worship leader, unction us to clap our hands, we patty cake God, and there are times where many straight rebel and not participate. But it is so important to participate in this act and even to clap when the Holy Spirit is leading. There is so much more that"s going in the spirit realm that we don"t even realize when we are clapping. In this Psalms we see that simply by clapping and shouting, God can magnify Himself to an even greater dominion, while releasing our inheritance among us.

CLAPS THAT SHAME THE ENEMY

Nahum 3:19

(KJV)
There is no healing of thy bruise; thy wound is grievous: all that hear the bruit of thee shall clap (taqa) the hands over thee: for upon whom hath not thy wickedness passed continually?

(God's Word)
There is no relief for your collapse. Your wound is fatal. All who hear the news about you will clap their hands. Who hasn't suffered from your endless evil?

In this chapter, Nineveh had been in defiance against God and He was making them aware of the sin they were committing against Him. They had been participating in witchcraft, whoredom, and murder, and God was threatening to bring a judgment of shame and death upon them for their sins. In this scripture, we see that the clap is used as an encore of the judgment that was to be sent against the city for their whoredom and idolatrous ways. It was used to increase shame for the sin they had committed. From this scripture, we can conclude that clapping can be used as an atmospheric weapon to enhance shame upon the wicked and the enemy, and to establish judgments done against the word and will of God.

RELEASING CLAPS OF ANGER, SCORN & GRIEF

Lamentations 2:15
(KJV)
All that pass by clap their hands at thee; they hiss and wag their head at the daughter of Jerusalem, saying, Is this the city that men call The perfection of beauty, The joy of the whole earth?

Numbers 24:10
(KJV)
And Balak's anger was kindled against Balaam, and he smote his hands together: and Balak said unto Balaam, I called thee to curse mine enemies, and, behold, thou hast altogether blessed them these three times.

In these passage of scripture above *Clap* means *Caphag* and is defined as:

1. to clap the hands for contempt
2. derision (the use of ridicule or scorn to show contempt)
3. grief
4. indignation (anger aroused at negative actions)
   5. punishment
6. rendered clap, smite, strike, suffice, and wallow

In Lamentations 2, the great nation of Jerusalem had been fallen due to sin. And those around them where clapping at them falling from the grace and prosperity of their heritage. The claps released against them caused scorn and ridicule and indignation as other nations where jealous of the favor of God on their lives so when they fell they clapped in triumph that Jerusalem was no longer the great nation God had destined them to be. We can learn a great lesson from this story and that is when we give into sin and worldliness, those around us that glory in our fall are further striking us with blows of contempt at the fate we have subjected ourselves to.

Unlike devils, God"s grace can be restored in our lives through repentance and turning from our wicked ways. Therefore, when translating the claps in these passages of scripture to weapons of warfare, we can use our clap to release anger, grief and derision, indignation, contempt, etc., against the enemy. The enemy will never repent. He"s always disobedient and fell from grace a long time ago. We therefore, can clap and release the glory of God over his fate of eternal damnation

In Numbers we see Balak attempting to use Balaam to curse Israel. Yet when Balaam saw that it pleased God to bless Israel, he continued to speak blessings over them. This made Balak very angry and He smote his hands together in indignation against Balaam. But in doing this, Balak ignited a war against God and the strike he sent again Balaam and curses he wanted to put upon Israel, became His own curse of shame and indignation. This is definitely revelation of how we can use our claps, our daggers for bad and they can become our own demise. Yet in considering clapping as an atmospheric weapon, we see that we can release

anger, scorn and indignation against the enemy
and the very curses he sends against us will
become his own mantle to bear.

THE CLAPPING PROPHET

Ezekiel 21:14-15
> *(KJV)*
> *Thou therefore, son of man, prophesy, and **smite
> thine hands together**, and let the sword be
> doubled the third time, the sword of the slain: it
> is the sword of the great men that are slain,
> which entereth into their privy chambers. I have
> set the point of the sword against all their gates,
> that [their] heart may faint, and [their] ruins be
> multiplied: ah! [it is] made bright, [it is]
> wrapped up for the slaughter.*

GOD ALMIGHTY CLAPPED

Ezekiel 21:16-17 *(KJV)*

> *Go thee one way or other, either on the right
> hand, or on the left, whithersoever thy face is set.
> I will also **smite mine hands together**, and I
> will cause my fury to rest: I the LORD have said
> it.*

Smite in these scriptures is *Nakah* and means:
to strike, smite, hit, beat, slay, kill
to be stricken or smitten
to beat, scourge, clap,
applaud, give a thrust to
smite, kill, slay (man or

beast) to smite, attack, attack
and destroy, conquer,
subjugate, ravage to smite,
chastise, send judgment
upon, punish, destroy to
receive a blow, be wounded,
beaten to be (fatally) smitten,
be killed, be slain
to be attacked and captured to be smitten (with
disease)
to be blighted (of plants)

In these passages of scripture, we see God
encouraging Ezekiel to clap and then God
almighty promises to also release a clap. The
reason God tells Ezekiel to clap is because He is
releasing a sword of judgment against those in
idolatry.

Ezekiel 21:8-11

> *(KJV)*
>
> *Again the word of the LORD came unto me,*
> *saying, Son of man, prophesy, and say, Thus*
> *saith the LORD; Say, A sword, a sword is*
> *sharpened, and also furbished: It is sharpened to*
> *make a sore slaughter; it is furbished that it may*
> *glitter: should we then make mirth? it*
> *contemneth the rod of my son, [as] every tree.*
> *And he hath given it to be furbished, that it may*
> *be handled: this sword is sharpened, and it is*
> *furbished, to give it into the hand of the slayer.*

The sword was more so a strong rebuke sent to
Israel to drive the people into a place of correction

and repentance and comes with an anointing of those in past generations that had to bring such words. Ezekiel's clapping in this scripture intensifies the sword (word) that is being released! It made the workings of God worse to the third degree such that the people have no choice but to turn and bow to the one true God.

So clearly we can discern from these scriptures the power of the clap; we see its ability to intensify whatever God releases to the third degree. Imagine the enemy coming against you and God fighting on your behalf. When you clap, the wrath of God and whatever else he releases to counterattack the enemy intensifies. Whewwwwwwww! And only His clap can cause what has been released through your clap to rest. As we see in *verse 17*, God is controlling the sword so that it will do only which it is sent. If God didn"t clap then the sword would have probably killed the Israelites so imagine what it does to the enemy. I would encourage you to read Ezekiel 21 for further foundation on this revelation.

2Kings 11-12
(KJV)
> *And he brought forth the king's son, and put the crown upon him, an gave him the testimony; and they made him king, and anointed him; and they clapped their hands, and said, God save the king.*

When reading this entire chapter of 2Kings 11, we discern that when Athaliah saw that her son was dead, she killed all the royal seed so that she would be king over Israel. But Jehosheba, the

87

daughter of king Joram, sister of Ahaziah, took Joash the son of Ahaziah, and stole him from among the king's sons who were slain. They hid him and his nurse in the bedchamber from Athaliah, so that he was not slain. He was hid for six years while Athaliah reigned over Israel. But in the seventh year, Joash was revealed and crowned as king over Israel.

Now we assume that in *verse 12*, the people were clapping because they were rejoicing and yet I am sure they were to an extent because Athaliah was wicked and they now had a new king who could restore the land.

However, clap in this passage of scripture means "*Nakah*" which is also the Hebrew word for *Smite* and means to strike, to kill, to chastise, to blow, etc. (see definition above). When reading this chapter, you will see that the guards and priests, etc., had set up an army of protection so the anointment service could go forth without Athaliah being able to overtake them and kill Joash. Therefore, the crowning indeed took place. When Athaliah heard the noise and the clapping of the hands she entered the temple, and was so appalled she rent her clothes and yelled "treason."

What Athaliah heard was not normal clapping. What Athaliah heard was judgment. She heard the smiting of her plans of being king being crushed. She was so wicked and wanted the throne so badly that she killed all those close to her to get it, or so she thought. The clapping was collapsing her self-made throne and casting her judgment. Needless to say she was put to death and so were those that followed her.

There are times when the Lord will lead me to clap while I am praying for a person. I can hear, sense, and sometimes see, demons fleeing and/or chains and bondages breaking off of them. Other times, the Lord will lead me to clap to open a portal or airway and to remove blockages in peoples" minds or soul or in the atmosphere, so that His presence can freely flow. Clapping is a serious kingdom weapon. It judges the enemy and kills his workings spiritually and naturally. Don't take it lightly as there is explosive demon demolishing power in your clap.

KINGDOM PROPS

Using Props to shift and change atmospheres, and to provide further prophetic revelation is very sufficient and bringing God's word to light (From *Prophetic Dance*, By Apostle Pamela Hardy). Examples of props from the *Prophetic Dance* article are as follows:

Sword   *Shield*   *Cloth*   *Bible Matte*
Tambourine
Candle   *Flags*   *Banners*   *Scepter Billows*
Crown

Because we will touch on some of these weapons throughout this book, we will only discuss one of these in this section, to provide a foundation of how God uses various props to shift atmospheres and establish the kingdom of heaven in the earth. We will begin with the signs and wonders God performed through Moses.

Moses is an excellent example that God uses props to demonstrate His expressions and workings. God gave Moses countless prophetic instructions that enabled him to demonstrate signs and wonders among Pharaoh and the people. These instructions encompassed the use of Moses" rod, and God even used the possession and deliverance of leprosy as a sign that He was speaking through Moses and using him to lead the Israelites out of Egypt.

God performed the acts above with Moses to give him an idea of how He would use him before King Pharaoh. I would describe King Pharaoh as the demonic king of slavery and the stronghold that prevents people from the promises and destiny of God. Despite God's warnings, he refused to let the Israelites go so they could walk in their destiny. Pharaoh was the king of Egypt. Egypt was a principality because it was a nation that was focused on personal gain and used God's people to do slave work. God used Moses to deliver the Israelites from this bondage. Therefore, as God performed various signs and wonders through Moses, He used him to save a nation. Now that's an atmosphere changer.

One of the major attributes God used Moses to change was unbelief in the people and in the atmosphere.

Exodus 4:2-9
(KJV)
And Moses answered and said, But, behold, they will not believe me, nor hearken unto my voice: for they will say, The LORD hath not appeared unto thee. And the LORD said unto him, What is that in thine hand? And he said, A rod. And he said, Cast it on the ground. And he cast it on the ground, and it became a serpent; and Moses fled from before it. And the LORD said unto Moses, Put forth thine hand, and take it by the tail. And he put forth his hand, and caught it, and it became a rod in his hand: That they may believe that the LORD God of their fathers, the

*God of Abraham, the God of Isaac, and the God
of Jacob, hath appeared unto thee.*

*And the LORD said furthermore unto him, Put
now thine hand into thy bosom. And he put his
hand into his bosom: and when he took it out,
behold, his hand was leprous as snow. And he
said, Put thine hand into thy bosom again. And
he put his hand into his bosom again; and
plucked it out of his bosom, and, behold, it was
turned again as his other flesh. And it shall
come to pass, if they will not believe thee, neither
hearken to the voice of the first sign, that they
will believe the voice of the latter sign. And it
shall come to pass, if they will not believe also
these two signs, neither hearken unto thy voice,
that thou shalt take of the water of the river, and
pour it upon the dry land: and the water which
thou takest out of the river shall become blood
upon the dry land.*

God could have chosen any prop to display His
miracles, signs and wonders to Pharaoh and all the
people. And truly being the Almighty God, He
didn't really need to use a rod at all as He simply
could have had Moses perform miracles and signs.
I however, sense that the rod was a representation
of God disciplining Pharaoh and his kingdom for
all the chastisement and punishment they had
bestowed upon His people. God was
demonstrating that He was the ultimate authority
and ruler of His people. That at any time, He had
the power to deliver them and there was nothing
Pharaoh could do about it. Each time Moses
performed a sign with the rod, God was exerting

His power and authority, while whipping the principalities, powers, and rulers that were connected to Pharaoh. God then toyed with Pharaoh as He would perform a mighty act through Moses then harden Pharaoh's heart so he wouldn't let Israel go. Pharaoh was so arrogant that he didn't realize he was being used by God to build the belief of the Israelites and to establish testimonies that we are still raving about today. God was simply using Pharaoh to make His name greater in the universe and at the end of Pharaoh's demise, God wasn't using Moses" rod, but the very hand of Moses to drown Pharaoh and his army His army in the red sea.

Exodus 14:21-31
(KJV)
And Moses stretched out his hand over the sea; and the LORD caused the sea to go [back] by a strong east wind all that night, and made the sea dry [land], and the waters were divided. And the children of Israel went into the midst of the sea upon the dry [ground]: and the waters [were] a wall unto them on their right hand, and on their left. And the Egyptians pursued, and went in after them to the midst of the sea, [even] all Pharaoh's horses, his chariots, and his horsemen.

And it came to pass, that in the morning watch the LORD looked unto the host of the Egyptians through the pillar of fire and of the cloud, and troubled the host of the Egyptians, And took off their chariot wheels, that they drave them heavily: so that the Egyptians said, Let us flee from the face of Israel; for the LORD fighteth for

*them against the Egyptians. And the LORD said
unto Moses, Stretch out thine hand over the sea,
that the waters may come again upon the
Egyptians, upon their chariots, and upon their
horsemen. And Moses stretched forth his hand
over the sea, and the sea returned to his strength
when the morning appeared; and the Egyptians
fled against it; and the LORD overthrew the
Egyptians in the midst of the sea. And the
waters returned, and covered the chariots, and
the horsemen, [and] all the host of Pharaoh that
came into the sea after them; there remained not
so much as one of them.*

*But the children of Israel walked upon dry [land]
in the midst of the sea; and the waters [were] a
wall unto them on their right hand, and on their
left. Thus the LORD saved Israel that day out of
the hand of the Egyptians; and
Israel saw the Egyptians dead upon the sea
shore. And Israel saw that great
work which the LORD did upon the Egyptians:
and the people feared the LORD, and believed
the LORD, and his servant Moses.*

There are instances the Lord will lead me to
minister with a rod. I call my rod, „*the demon
buster.*" There is no power in the rod, but when
God leads me to minister with it, I know He is
providing a physical prophetic display that He is
judging principalities, powers, rulers of darkness,
etc., and He is letting it be publically displayed that
He is chastising, pushing and judging darkness. It
is important however, to allow the Lord to lead
you when using props. Another thing we learn

from Moses as well is if the prop is use inappropriately, it can yield great consequences. We discern this from Numbers 20, when Moses was upset because the Israelites where murmuring and complaining about being hungry and thirsty and not having faith in God. Moses anger was legitimate but his act of striking the rock in anger wasn't, as his actions didn't bring honor to God. Even though he performed a miracle of bringing water from the rock and countless miracles before and after this one, using his rod inappropriately cost him the promise land.

Numbers 20:10-12

(KJV)

And Moses and Aaron gathered the congregation together before the rock, and he said unto them, Hear now, ye rebels; must we fetch you water out of this rock? And Moses lifted up his hand, and with his rod he smote the rock twice: and the water came out abundantly, and the congregation drank, and their beasts [also]. And the LORD spake unto Moses and Aaron, Because ye believed me not, to sanctify me in the eyes of the children of Israel, therefore ye shall not bring this congregation into the land which I have given them.

As atmosphere changers we have to handle the things of God with great care and exhibit His character when we are before the people. This is essential in Him getting proper and due glory out of everything we do in His name.

FLAG MINISTRY! UNSPOKEN POWER

Flags represent a bold statement that we worship and serve the true and living God. When we wave a flag we are saying who we represent without even opening our mouth. We aren't just saying it to the congregation, but people passing by, the grave, hell, the heavenlies, demons, principalities, the angels, and to God.

One becomes a gatekeeper to the atmosphere when waving a flag and has the ability to open any door, gate, or window in the spirit realm. There is an authority that comes with its declaration. It gives you the ability to cleanse the atmosphere of any demonic oppression or possession and release into the atmosphere whatever is needed for God's presence to manifest with miracles, signs, and wonders.

When ministering with flags, search out what is needed in the atmosphere at that time and ask God what flag is needed to wave to make that word flesh. While you are waving the flag, make declarations into the heavenlies about who God is and command that window, door, or gate to open.

Merriam Webster Online Dictionary defines _Window_:

1. an opening especially in the wall of a building for admission of light and air that is usually closed by casements or sashes containing

transparent material (as glass) and capable of being opened and shut
2. Windowpane, a space behind a window of a retail store containing displayed merchandise
3. an opening in a partition or wall through which business is conducted
4. a means of entrance or access; *especially* : a means of obtaining information

Merriam Webster Online Dictionary defines *Door*:
1. a usually swinging or sliding barrier by which an entry is closed and opened;
2. a similar part of a piece of furniture, doorway
3. a means of access or participation, opportunity

Merriam Webster Online Dictionary defines *Gate:*
1. an opening in a wall or fence
2. a city or castle entrance often with defensive structures (as towers)
3. the frame or door that closes a gate, a movable barrier
4. a means of entrance or exit, starting gate
5. an area for departure or arrival
6. a space between two markers through which a competitor must pass in the course of a slalom race

Let's say spirit of heaviness was in the atmosphere and we wanted to use the flags to combat it. First I would encourage choosing a flag that represents praise and joy and would declare that against that oppression. I would suggest that while waving the flag, battering in prayer against the spirit. Command it to be dislodged and for a doorway to praise and joy to open in the spirit realm. Also, asking the Holy Spirit to come guide you as you are waving the flag is essential as He will show you or have you wave the flag in certain ways where it would become an effective weapon within the spirit realm. At times when using flags, we can use several flags or one significant flag. It is important to understand that as atmosphere changers, we gain ground by moving. Therefore, unless the Lord leads, it's best not to just stand in place when waving a flag. Our feet can aid in treading upon the enemy and further taking over the atmosphere for God.

Some at times, feel lead to dance with the flag, or sway from side to side, or circle the sanctuary with it, or walk up and down the aisle, vortex style. But whatever God leads you to do be obedient. Let Him lead you in movements that demonstrate what you are declaring to the heavenlies. In addition, I would suggest making sure one's facial and body is in line with the declaration you are presenting as you are engaged in flag ministry. When soldiers go to war and hold up their flag, they don't stand there trembling or looking fearful. Is there life at stake? Yes! Could they die? Yes! But when they hold up that flag they are saying I am a representative of my country and I come to fight till I am sent back home, die, or win the war. That is the kind of mentality we have to have when we wave our flags for Jesus. We are there to take over the atmosphere and expel any demonic force that is striving to hinder the move of God, while declaring that He IS LORD, NOW AND FOREVERMORE! We aren't there to negotiate with demons, or even with those who don't want to worship, or want flags waving over their heads. We are decreeing that Jesus is the *Prince of Peace* and we will worship Him and give Him due glory.

Please take into consideration that just like a soldier in the army, if you don't want to fight, or really are just waving the flag because you were told to or just to be doing something, that you have the potential to get yourself killed and those around you. You put your spirit and others in a vulnerable position to be overtaken by the enemy.

Gatekeepers are watchman on the wall and watchmen do not sleep on the job. They do not half do their job. If they do, someone sneaks through the gate and ends up taking over the city. If you half do your ministry when waving the flags, then you are letting demons hang out in your midst or you are allow the enemy to have ground and territory that God is saying is yours. You are also giving other demonic forces the opportunity to come in and further bind up the presence of God. It is essential to be alert and work on having a keen sensitivity to what is going on in the atmosphere so that every demon can be exposed and cast out and the gates are secure so only what is of God can gain entrance.

This section regarding flags was written by Kathy Williams of New Day Ministries, Muncie IN.

Flags establish a nation's identity.

Flags establish that victory has been won and territory has been taken.

Flags establish the identity of the conquering troops.

Flags identify intentions, whether good or bad, such as this Pirate flag.

Anyone who sees this Red Cross flag anywhere in the world knows that it means medicine and provisions. Those that operate under this flag can go anywhere in the world at any time and be received. They can step into the middle of a battlefield and EXPECT not to be harmed.

Planting a flag is a statement of achieving a goal for the greater good of your nation.

Flags represent taking territory!

Maybe what some of you have not experienced is
that when the flags are waving in the service,
and it gets quiet, you can hear the flags
whipping the air. Oh, I long for the day that
worship permits us to go to the place where you
can only hear the flags altogether breaking the
atmosphere and hear the whipping sounds. Oh,
yes Lord!

Do you know that flags can measure the winds?

Now think about that in the spirit realm?

> **Psalm 20:5** *We will rejoice in thy salvation, and
> in the name of our God we will set up our
> **banners**: the LORD fulfill all thy petitions.*

> **Psalm 60:4** *Thou hast given a **banner** to them
> that fear thee, that it may be displayed because of
> the truth. Selah.*

Song of Solomon 2:4 *He brought me to the banqueting house, and his **banner** over me was love.*

Song of Solomon 6:4 *Thou art beautiful, O my love, as Tirzah, comely as Jerusalem, terrible as an army with **banners**.*

Song of Solomon 6:10 *Who is she that looketh forth as the morning, fair as the moon, clear as the sun, and terrible as an army with **banners**?*

Isaiah 13:2 *Lift ye up a **banner** upon the high mountain, exalt the voice unto them, shake the hand, that they may go into the gates of the nobles.*

Banner is *Dagal* which means to be conspicuous, to look, to behold, to set up a standard.

Another word the scripture uses is *Nec* which is something lifted up, standard, signal, signal pole, ensign, banner, sign, sail. It"s primitive root is *Nacac* which is to be lifted up or displayed. Some scripture references include:

Zechariah 9:16	ensign
Numbers 21:8	pole
Numbers 26:10	sign
Psalm 60:4	banner
Isaiah 49:22	standard
Ezekiel 27:7	sail

A third Hebrew term is *Oth* which means a signal and can mean proof of a miracle. The most famous of these is in Genesis 9:12 when God tells Noah that He is setting a bow in the sky as a token or an *Oth* that set covenant between God and mankind.

HEALING & GLORY MANTLES

As we continue to see, God will use the most interesting methods to show forth His glory, shift atmospheres and manifest His promises in the earth. He will use His words, the laying of hands; healing someone without anyone touching them, His presence, music, His word, handkerchiefs, aprons, clothes, His breath, our shadows, etc. God is so unique and loves to manifest unexplainable manifestations of who He is. The healing and glory mantles are just another method He has given us as atmosphere changers to manifest His healing and soaking presence and show forth His power in an exquisite manner.

Acts 5:12-16

> *(KJV)*
> *And through the hands of the apostles many signs and wonders were done among the people. And they were all with one accord in Solomon's Porch. Yet none of the rest dared join them, but the people esteemed them highly. And believers were increasingly added to the Lord, multitudes of both men and women, so that they brought the sick out into the streets and laid them on beds and couches, that at least the shadow of Peter passing by might fall on some of them. Also a multitude gathered from the surrounding cities to Jerusalem, bringing sick*

people and those who were tormented by
unclean spirits, and they were all healed.

Acts 19:11-12
(KJV)
Now God worked unusual miracles by the hands
of Paul, so that even handkerchiefs or aprons
were brought from his body to the sick, and the
diseases left them and the evil spirits went out of
them.

Even as God performed *"SPECIAL MIRACLES by*
the hands of Paul," we know as well, He desires to
use us in the area of greater works for His glory.

Mathew 10:7:8
(KJV)
And as ye go, preach, saying, the kingdom of
heaven is at hand. Heal the sick, cleanse the
lepers, raise the dead, cast out devils: freely ye
have received, freely give.

John 14:12
(KJV)
Verily, verily, I say unto you, He that believeth
on me, the works that I do shall he do also; and
greater [works] than these shall he do; because I
go unto my Father.

During Bible times, a handkerchief was used for
wrapping the head of a corpse for burial. With
that being said, just imagine what an anointed
105

handkerchief can do for the living or even someone that God wants raised from the dead. I am sure that handkerchief could bring the dead back to life, resurrect dead dreams, visions, desires, destinies, and on and on.

The Handkerchief in the bible days wasn't fancy. It was simply an apron like you see a blacksmith or other workers wear. That's because it isn't about the handkerchief itself, but the anointing of God that manifests through it, which causes His healing power to manifest.

In our dance ministry, we call our healing shawl/mantle, the *Mishkan*. The *Mishkan* was derived from one of our dance mentors. She was ironing her curtains one day and the Lord told her to dance with them. She obeyed the voice of the Lord and this has been a part of her ministry ever since. God uses her to bring healing and His prophetic presence into a place using what she was calling "the curtain." I laughed at her and expressed that she couldn't go around the world calling her healing mantle a curtain so myself and another dancer conducted a personal Bible study and God lead us to name the curtain, the "*Mishkan*." Our dance mentor loved the name, and its biblical foundation, which added even more grace and power of how God uses this tool for His glory.

In the Old Testament, the presence in the tabernacle was known as the

Shekinah Glory. The "*Shekinah Glory*" is the Hebrew expression for the "*Very Presence of God*". Though the word *Shekinah* is not in the bible, it a derivative and does indeed occur often in scripture through the translated word, "*Dwell*" and all throughout the bible, we see God's Shekinah glory dwelling among His people.

Exodus 24:16

(KJV)

And Moses went up into the mount, and a cloud covered the mount. And the glory of the LORD abode upon mount Sinai, and the cloud covered it six days: and the seventh day he called unto Moses out of the midst of the cloud.

Verse 40:35 (KJV)
And the sight of the glory of the LORD [was] like devouring fire on the top of the mount in the eyes of the children of Israel. And Moses went into the midst of the cloud, and gat him up into the mount: and Moses was in the mount forty days and forty nights.

Numbers 9:17-18

(KJV)

And on the day that the tabernacle was reared up the cloud covered the tabernacle, namely, the tent of the testimony: and at even there was upon the tabernacle as it were the appearance of fire, until the morning. So it was always: the cloud covered it by day, and the appearance of fire by night. And when the cloud was taken up from the tabernacle, then after that the children of Israel journeyed: and in the place where the

*cloud abode, there the children of Israel pitched
their tents. At the commandment of the LORD
the children of Israel journeyed, and at the
commandment of the LORD they pitched: as
long as the cloud abode upon the tabernacle they
rested in their tents. 19 And when the cloud
tarried long upon the tabernacle many days,
then the children of Israel kept the charge of the
LORD, and journeyed not.*

2Chronicles 7:1-2

(KJV)

*Now when Solomon had made an end of praying,
the fire came down from heaven, and consumed
the burnt offering and the sacrifices; and the
glory of the LORD filled the house. And the
priests could not enter into the house of the
LORD, because the glory of the LORD had filled
the LORD'S house.*

Luke 2:9

(KJV)

*And, lo, the angel of the Lord came upon them,
and the glory of the Lord shone round about
them: and they were sore afraid.*

From those scriptures, we see that God"s presence,
His Shekinah desires to dwell among us. He loves
when we create a place for Him to dwell and in the
Old Testament, they had what was known as the
Tabernacle or Tent of Meetings.

Tabernacle in the Hebrew is *Mishkan* and means:

1. the dwelling place or dwellings

108

2. Him who dwells

The primitive root word for *Tabernacle* is *Shakan/Shekinah* and means:

1. to settle down, abide, dwell, tabernacle, reside
2. to settle down to abide
3. to abide, dwell, reside
4. to make settle down, establish
5. to make or cause to dwell
6. to lay, place, set, establish, settle, fix
7. to cause to dwell or abide

Revelations 21:2-3

> *(KJV)*
> *Then I, John, saw the holy city, New Jerusalem, coming down out of heaven from God, prepared as a bride adorned for her husband. And I heard a loud voice from heaven saying, "Behold, the tabernacle (the Mishkan) of God is with men, and He will dwell with them, and they shall be His people. God Himself will be with them and be their God.*

When the *Mishkan*, God's dwelling manifests, He seeks to inhabit everything about us and establish His glory in our midst. God rend the heavens with His most violent, and awesome presence, that seeks to consume our minds, our perceptions, our religious jargon, our rules, and regulations. He comes to shake and elevate everything we know about Him or think we know about Him. He uses His presence to trigger our hunger for more so that we combat those things that may not be like Him, while seeking a greater depth of Him, where He doesn't just visit but live and abide among us.

During my prayer time, I soak my *Mishkan* in the presence of the Lord, while asking His Shekinah Glory to inhabit it so that when I minister it heals, delivers, saturates, dismantles strongholds, and set the captives free. One fascinating way I have seen God manifest as I minister with the *Mishkan* and healing shawls, is administering His love to people.

Sometimes, the Lord will have us go out into the crowd and wrap people in the mantle and deliverance begins to manifests as they are wrapped in His presence. There are also instances where the Lord will have me minister with the *Mishkan* and I am slapping demons with it and dismantling strongholds, or clearing a place out from demonic manifestation so that His purity and righteousness can come and invade the atmosphere. Many times, I am hesitant when God directs me to minister with the *Mishkan* because I rarely am released to minister the glory dances with it as usually He leads me in warfare, or I am hesitant because I don't want to hit someone or knock over stuff. I am sure I have hit some people, though I haven't knocked over anything that I know of just yet. However, I have seen God perform unexplainable miracles with the *Mishkan* and healing shawls that is far more worth any embarrassment I would endure. If God leads you to pray over a handkerchief or scarf and give it to someone, by all means do so. If He leads you to add a healing or glory mantle to your ministry, be obedient. They are a part of the greater works He desires to manifest in us for His glory.

HEALING BILLOWS

Our group first saw the billow in operation when attending the Eagles International Dance Institutes" conference. It was the most beautiful flowing material that literally ushered the raining/reigning presence of God. As it billowed up and down, it felt/feels like a liquid healing raining from heaven. We inquired about what the beautiful cloth was from one of the venders at the conference, and we were told it was called a *billow*. We purchased a billow from their ministry and incorporated this instrument into our Sunday morning worship and have since then made our own billows, to which people have experienced great refreshing, deliverance, breakthrough and the miracle working power of God.

Psalms 42:7

(KJV)

*Deep calleth unto deep at the noise of thy waterspouts: all thy waves and thy **billows** are gone over me.*

John 2:3

(KJV)

*For thou hadst cast me into the deep, in the midst of the seas; and the floods compassed me about: all thy **billows** and thy waves passed over me.*

Billow in the Hebrew is *Gal* and means:

1. heap, spring, wave, billow
2. heap (of stones)
3. over dead body, alone
4. used in ratifying a covenant
5. waves (fig. of chastisement of Jehovah)
6. spring

The billow is the heaping waves of God's glory. It symbolizes covenant of the former rain and the later rain. It is God raining down like the spring season with His harvest and refreshing.

Jeremiah 5:24
(KJV)

They do not say in their heart, "Let us now fear the Lord our God, Who gives rain, both the former and the latter, in its season. He reserves for us the appointed weeks of the harvest.

Hosea 6:3
(KJV)

Let us know, Let us pursue the knowledge of the Lord. His going forth is established as the morning; He will come to us like the rain, Like the latter and former rain to the earth.

Joel 2:23
(KJV)

Be glad then, you children of Zion, And rejoice in the Lord your God; For He has given you the former rain faithfully, And He will cause the

rain to come down for you – The former rain,
And the latter rain in the first month.

The billow is great for demonstrating the tangible presence of the Lord. It is also excellent for manifesting God's healing and deliverance anointing. As the billow is waved, people will gather under it to soak and be refreshed in the tangible presence of the Lord. It also strengthens corporate worship as people join together to kneel and lay prostrate before God.

COLORS SPEAK

Understanding colors and what they represent is very important as an atmosphere changer, especially when interpreting dreams and visions and acquiring further clarity as a seer in the spirit realm. Often times, God will require you to wear a specific color or show you a specific color to identify, demonstrate or explain what He is speaking to or for His people.

The definitions below were acquired from the article entitled, *"Prophetic Dance,"* By Apostle Pamela Hardy.

> Gold – The Deity of Christ (One of the Colors of the Tabernacle,
> Exodus 28)
> Silver – Redemption
> Bronze – Refinement
> Black – Death, Famine, Peril
> Green – Everlasting Life, Prosperity
> Purple - Royalty
> Scarlet – The Passion of Christ, His Humanity
> Blue – Heavenly Things, Refreshing River, Holy Spirit
> Red – The blood of Jesus
> Rainbow – Covenant
> White – Holiness, Purity, Light, Righteousness

The rainbow is a perfect Biblical example of how God uses colors to express His feelings and establish His will in the earth realm. After destroying all the earth accept that which was in Noah's ark, God made a covenant with Noah that He would never again destroy the earth with water. He expressed to Noah that the rainbow would be a symbol that He had made this covenant with Him. Genesis 9 reads:

> And I, behold, I establish my covenant with you, and with your seed after you; And with every living creature that [is] with you, of the fowl, of the cattle, and of every beast of the earth with you; from all that go out of the ark, to every beast of the earth. And I will establish my covenant with you; neither shall all flesh be cut off any more by the waters of a flood; neither shall there any more be a flood to destroy the earth.
> And God said, This [is] the token of the covenant which I make between me and you and every living creature that [is] with you, for perpetual generations: I do set my bow in the cloud, and it shall be for a token of a covenant between me and the earth. And it shall come to pass, when I bring a cloud over the earth, that the bow shall be seen in the cloud:
>
> And I will remember my covenant, which [is] between me and you and every living creature of all flesh; and the waters shall no more become a flood to destroy all flesh. And the bow shall be in the cloud; and I will look upon it, that I may remember the everlasting covenant between God and every living creature of all flesh that [is] upon the earth.

115

The rainbow was a colorful atmospheric symbol of God's covenant with man and beast that He would not destroy the earth again with water. There are occasions God will tell me or give me visions of colors to wear for ministry as a demonstration of what He desires to establish in a place or the people. He has had me wear purple as a symbol of releasing royalty. Frequently my pastor will wear certain colors and many of us can sense when she is about to minister a convicting word on sin, or a message on purity, etc. Her ministry garments tend to provide an idea of her message before she even speaks a word and we just gear ourselves up for the altar call.

Often as atmosphere changes we will see colors in the sky or in visions and dreams and negate their meaning. It is essential to consider whether God is speaking and what He is saying during these times as it could be a prophetic or atmospheric symbol or word from the Lord. In the instance with the rainbow, God made an everlasting covenant with all flesh. I wonder what covenants and blessings we have missed by not being more susceptible to God speaking to us through symbols and colors.

KINGDOM POETRY

David is our greatest example of how God uses prophetic poetry.

Psalms 45:1 declares:

(KJV)
My heart is indicting a good matter: I speak of the things which I have made touching the king: my tongue is the pen of a ready writer.

(The Message)
My heart bursts its banks, spilling beauty and goodness. I pour it out in a poem to the king, shaping the river into words:

(NIV)
My heart overflows with a beautiful thought! I will recite a lovely poem to the king, for my tongue is like the pen of a skillful poet.

David had a love for expressing the awesomeness of God. His Psalms are atmospheric declarations that not only proclaim and reveal the presence of God they are also prophetic utterances that are still coming to past today. Just like David"s poetry, our writings can be used to bring a word of encouragement, answer a question from God, express the thoughts, heart and intents of God, establish who we are and who God is, prophecy our future, the fate of the enemy, our victories, etc. Moreover, poetry can be used to compare and contrast biblical and personal experiences as there are moments where our dance ministry will use poetry to set the tone for a dance or dramatization. Though this is rarely utilized, I believe that poetry and even prophetic declarations would be excellent for opening and setting the atmosphere of a service and establishing the presence and workings of God. David said *"his heart was indicting a good matter."*

Indicting in the Hebrew is *Rachash* and means: to keep moving, stir

Good in the Hebrew is *Tomb* and means:
1. good, pleasant, agreeable
2. pleasant, agreeable (to the senses)
3. pleasant (to the higher nature)
4. good, excellent (of its kind)
5. good, rich, valuable in estimation
6. good, appropriate, becoming
7. better (comparative)
8. glad, happy, prosperous (of man's sensuous nature)
9. good understanding (of man's intellectual nature)
10. good, kind, benign
11. welfare, prosperity, happiness

David was saying that his heart was excited about speaking forth the matters God was leading Him

to write. He was eager to share and declare them.
They were pleasant, agreeable, and in line with the
welfare and prosperity that God had ordained for
him and his kingdom so he enjoyed recording and
sharing them.

Often I will send care packages to people and
include poetry and declarations that have often
yielded encouragement and answers to life
struggles, so do not hesitate if God is leading you
to share your poetry with someone, write a poem
or declaration for a person or to use it in your
ministry. I even encourage that as God leads you
to write, ask Him who should be blessed by it and
how should it be used in your ministry. Your
poetry could be the weapon to unlocking doors in
a person's life, in a church, community, and as
David often did, in a nation.

PROPHETIC ART

In the beginning, God created the heavens and the earth. He saw that the earth was dark, without form and void. God used His presence as a paint brush and moved so eloquently across the world birthing forth color and radiance and causing light and life to a dead world. God took time, six days, in structuring and strategically positioning each portion of the universe. Everything that God created is a work of art and reveals a portion of who He is and what He is made of. From the beautiful skies, to the elegance in the seasons of the year, to the awesomeness of oceans, rivers, windy trees, we see God's perfect art at work all around us. Even our very presence is a structure of God's praise for the word says *we were made in his image (Gen 1:27) and that we were fearfully and wonderfully made (Psa 139:14)*. Why even after God made male and female, he spoke forth a prophetic declaration that would follow us till all eternity. He said in *Genesis 1:27,*

> *(KJV)*
> *Be fruitful, and multiply, and replenish the earth, and subdue it: and have dominion over the fish of the sea, and over the fowl of the air, and over every living thing that moveth upon the earth.*

And we are not even going to get into how God structured the tabernacle and Aarons garments, etc. and how prophetic His workings were to the coming and fulfillment of Christ!

Prophetic art is a seer weapon as it is conveyed through the eyes and visual imagination of a person. Prophetic art can be sculptures or the building of something. It can be paintings expressed using oil, watercolor, pencil, pastels, ink, crayons, or a sculpture of clay or metal, magazine scraps, multimedia collages, etc. With the advance of technology, people are now able to use their gifting in the areas of graphic designs which has been a blessing when creating book covers, posters, logos, advertising church services and programs, sharing church announcements, etc.

Essentially prophetic art can be used to express the heart and vision of
God, speak forth His oracles, express His strategies, reveal His timetables and judgments, evangelize the lost, and teach a biblical word. I have seen people use this gift during services and what God reveals through them shifts the atmosphere and help bring forth wisdom that establishes people and spheres. For those who are visual, prophetic art is a great way to further share revelation and knowledge God is speaking and establishing.

WEAPON OF SPEAKING IN TONGUES

Many times we go into the enemy's camp and we are all hyped about taking back what the devil has stolen, but right in the middle of the battle, we become weary, frustrated, tired and even physically out of breath. We mean well and desire to war and intercede against the enemy, and truly give our all, but while others are still battling and their spirit is moving in full force, some find themselves eventually watching instead of participating in the battle. Others are still in the spirit, wreaking havoc in the devil's camp, while the pooped saint is catching his or her breath. Their bodies are zonked because their spirit has worn out and often, they aren't even sure the reason they aren't able to sustain or remain in the battle. Generally the reason for this is because:

1. We cannot war or intercede with our mind!
2. We cannot war or intercede with our emotions!
3. We cannot war or intercede with our flesh!
4. We cannot war or intercede with reasoning!
5. We cannot war or intercede with our intellect!
6. WE MUST WAR OR INTERCEDE WITH AND THROUGH OUR SPIRIT!

Ephesians 6 :10-15 contends:

(Message)

And that about wraps it up. God is strong, and he wants you strong. So take everything the Master has set out for you, well-made weapons of the best materials. And put them to use so you will be able to stand up to everything the Devil throws your way. This is no afternoon athletic contest that we'll walk away from and forget about in a couple of hours. This is for keeps, a life-or-death fight to the finish against the Devil and all his angels.

Be prepared. You're up against far more than you can handle on your own. Take all the help you can get, every weapon God has issued, so that when it's all over but the shouting you'll still be on your feet. Truth, righteousness, peace, faith, and salvation are more than words. Learn how to apply them. You'll need them throughout your life. God's Word is an indispensable weapon. **In the same way, prayer is essential in this ongoing warfare.**
Pray hard and long. Pray for your brothers and sisters. Keep your eyes open. Keep each other's spirits up so that no one falls behind or drops out.

It is our spirit, the Holy Spirit within us that we discussed in the previous chapter that leads us in shifting atmospheres and establishing God"'s climate. Though our bodies and minds have a tendency to become weak, our spirit is willing and very capable to sustaining the anointing and calling of God on our life. Especially, when we

have exercised our prayer life, and learned how to
pray hard and long as the word above is
encouraging us to do.

Matthew 26:40-45 reads:

(Amplified)
*And He came to the disciples and found them
sleeping, and He said to Peter, What! Are you so
utterly unable to stay awake and keep watch
with Me for one hour? All of you must keep
awake (give strict attention, be cautious and
active) and watch and pray, that you may not
come into temptation. The spirit indeed is
willing, but the flesh is weak. Again a second
time He went away and prayed, My Father, if
this cannot pass by unless I drink it, Your will
be done. And again He came and found them
sleeping, for their eyes were weighed down with
sleep. So, leaving them again, He went away
and prayed for the third time, using the same
words. Then He returned to the disciples and
said to them, Are you still sleeping and taking
your rest? Behold, the hour is at hand, and the
Son of Man is betrayed into the hands of
especially wicked sinners whose way or nature it
is to act in opposition to God].*

(The Message)
*When he came back to his disciples, he found
them sound asleep. He said to Peter, "Can't you
stick it out with me a single hour? Stay alert; be
in prayer so you don't wander into temptation
without even knowing you're in danger. There is
a part of you that is eager, ready for anything in
God. But there's another part that's as lazy as
an old dog sleeping by the fire." He then left*

*them a second time. Again he prayed, "My
Father, if there is no other way than this,
drinking this cup to the dregs, I'm ready. Do it
your way." When he came back, he again found
them sound asleep. They simply couldn't keep
their eyes open. This time he let them sleep on,
and went back a third time to pray, going over
the same ground one last time. When he came
back the next time, he said, "Are you going to
sleep on and make a night of it? My time is up,
the Son of Man is about to be handed over to the
hands of sinners. Get up! Let's get going! My
betrayer is here."*

Jesus was attempting to express to the disciples
that they were in a spiritual battle and that it was
dangerous to fall asleep in the middle of a fight.
The disciples however, understood that it was
important to be fervent for God, however, their
spirit was hungry to do His will, but there flesh
was weak. So despite, Jesus waking them up a
couple of times, they still continued to fall asleep.

Imagine being in the army of the USA and being
sent to war. You are on the battleground and
shooting is going on all around you, yet the
soldiers fighting with you begin to fall asleep right
there in the midst of the battle. What would you
do? This happens in the body of Christ all the
time. It happens often during praise and worship
and intercessory prayer. We will be right at the
brink of defeating the enemy and taking back what
he has stolen, then our cohorts become weary and
stop praising, worshipping, declaring, or their
natural bodies weaken right in the midst of the

battle. This is very dangerous not only for the person that is sleeping but for the people who are still warring, praying, praising, etc., because it provides an open door for the enemy to counterattack and either beat us down or regain ground that we have just conquered.

In order to be efficient atmosphere changers, one must be filled with the Holy Spirit and one must develop an effective and fervent prayer life, and be a living witness and instrument in knowledge and example of God's word. I also want to encourage you that if you do not speak in tongues that you ask God to manifest His prayer language in you.

I was raised Baptist and didn't believe and understand speaking in tongues. And people often told me I wasn't filled with the Holy Spirit because I didn't speak in tongues, yet God would use me to release healing and deliverance to these peoples" lives. I was therefore, very hurt by their comments and it made me not really want to speak in tongues. But one day God revealed to me that it wasn't that I didn't have His Holy Spirit, but that I was denying myself greater power by not allowing His voice and presence to be fully activated through me. He then sent a couple of people to me that confirmed this and provided further revelation of the benefits of speaking in tongues, and then I begin to ask Him to manifest His voice and Spirit in me in a greater measure. One day while praying with my Godmother, I begin to sing in tongues and a few days later began to speak in tongues. That has been years ago, and now I love speaking in tongues so much that I pray for fun and sometimes pray in my sleep (laughing but very serious). I must admit that my entire life changed and God's power operating in me has gone leaps and bounds since I am able to build and esteem others and myself using my prayer language.

Furthermore, misinterpretation of the scriptures tends to shun people from speaking in tongues. But *1Corinthians 14* is actually about making sure we represent and honor God among those who may not understand how He operates. It truly is no different than what we discussed in the previous chapter when Moses became angry and struck the rock. The miracle of water manifested, but he didn't honor God or present the character of God. Speaking in tongues has to be done with decency so that nonbelievers or the believers who don't speak in their prayer language yet, won't misunderstand it and fear pursuing it. However, God eagerly desires us to use our prayer language even during church services. Additionally, He desires us to have a clear understanding of His Spirit so we can encourage others to pursue all He entails. I therefore, admonish you to study the scriptures and ask God for a personal revelation on the fruit of speaking in your prayer language.

As atmosphere changers the most efficient way to build up our spirit man is to have a consistent prayer life and be a student of the word. This enables us to sufficiently stand in the gap for ourselves and for others, and it teaches us how to hear God's voice, be obedient to His word, know His promises and commandments, and be led by the Holy Spirit in our prayers.

Lets" discuss effectively praying through the Holy Spirit rather than our emotions. At times, we will hear the preacher say we are about to go into the enemy's camp and take back what the devil has stolen. We are eager to engage because we are mad at the devil and ready for war. But instead of shifting to our spirit, we pray out of our emotions and minds. We pray from an aspiration to see breakthrough or desire to be victorious rather than knowing we are already victorious, and are just acting out and pulling out of the spirit, what has already been loosed to us in heaven.

When we pray in this manner, our minds are often replaying scenes and conversations from our day, or what we have to do that day, or replaying scenes of emotional frustration concerning situations or regarding the enemy. It tends to draw our minds into some emotional agitation, frustration, or burdens we are experiencing. Therefore, right in the middle of prayer, we wander off to another subject and we begin praying for something else or not at all, instead of sticking with the original assignment at hand. This is dangerous and a NO! NO! You run the risk of defeating or aborting the mission when praying in this manner. It also jeopardizes those who are praying with you as it causes a division that allows the attacks of the enemy to gain ground among your camp.

The most effective way to pray when you are interceding and/or contending is to use your prayer language to pray from your loins...your loins are in your stomach area.

Ephesians 6:14 states:
(KJV)
Stand therefore, having your loins girt about with truth, and having on the breastplate of righteousness;
(Amplified)
Stand therefore [hold your ground], having tightened the belt of truth around your loins and having put on the breastplate of integrity and of moral rectitude and right standing with God,

Your loins are the part of your human body on each side of the spinal column between the hipbone and the false ribs. The reason I state this is because,

Romans 8:26-28 reads:
(KJV)
Likewise the Spirit also helpeth our infirmities: for we know not what we should pray for as we ought: but the Spirit itself maketh intercession for us with groanings which cannot be uttered. And he that searcheth the hearts knoweth what is the mind of the Spirit, because he maketh intercession for the saints according to the will of God. And we know that all things work together for good to them that love God, to them who are the called according to his purpose.

This type of prayer derives from your loin area as you pray in tongues. You will know you are praying from this position because you will feel a pulling, tenseness or even sometimes a pouring out from your stomach. The reason why it is essential to pray from here is because this is where the generative power of the Holy Spirit is said to reside. This is where your spirit is. Generative power is the Hebrew definition of *loins*. So when you pray from here, you are praying from your spirit, which causes one's mind and body to line up and be in order with the assignment at hand. A person will not give out easy when consistently praying from their loins, as when praying from this area of your body, it is constantly spiritually reproducing power to sustain you and keep your mind and body fresh and from wearing out in the battle.

Many only want to pray in their prayer language when they "feel God." They have been taught that it isn't God speaking through them unless they go through an emotional and physical RELIGIOUS ritual that is said to be the determent factor that God has now manifested and is with them. However, this is a lie from the pit of hell and is a tactic the devil has used against saints to keep us from starting the battle off effectively being lead of the Holy Spirit. While we trying to conjure up God's spirit, the devil is laughing and shooting missiles at us.

The word says in John 4:23, *"we are to worship in spirit and in truth."* This means we should have a daily walk in the spirit. There is nothing to conjure up as God is already with us and manifested in us, and our daily walk with Him is our proof that He is eternally manifested in and with us.

The word Stand in Ephesians 6:14 is _Histemi_ and means:

1. to cause or make to stand, to place, put, set
2. to bid to stand by, [set up]
3. in the presence of others, in the midst, before judges, before members of the Sanhedrin;
4. to place, to make firm, fix establish
5. to cause a person or a thing to keep his or its place
6. to stand, be kept intact (of family, a kingdom), to escape in safety
7. to establish a thing, cause it to stand
8. to uphold or sustain the authority or force of anything
9. to set or place in a balance
10. continue safe and sound, stand unharmed, to stand ready or prepared
11. to be of a steadfast mind
12. of quality, one who does not hesitate, does not waiver

The loins are where the truth of God resides. It is where the power of God resides. Praying from the loins produces power to stand in the unwavering truth of God. It also dispels religious rituals as it shifts us directly to the spirit realm and dismantles the lies and deceptions of the enemy. This is because, when praying from our loins we are standing in the promises and commandments of God. We are standing in the truth and balance of God. We are fixed and established and are no longer wavering like we would if we were praying from our minds or emotions. We are not reasoning with the devil and intellectualizing the plan God has given us. We are not wandering off in our thoughts due to praying through our emotions, hype, and intellect. We aren't standing in the midst of the battle tired and weary in our physical bodies while watching others continue fervently. Yet as we pray from our loins we exert the spiritual stamina to remain in the battle and fight the good fight of faith and manifesting victory in our midst.

When utilizing our generative loin power, it causes everything about us to immediately come into subjecting of the spirit of God within us. Our thoughts, will, mind, intellect, reasoning, physical and mortal bodies, line up with the will of God. We are not trying to strike up a fight with our RELIGIOUS rituals and emotions and intellect; yet we throw the first punch, launch the first missile, causing confusion to the enemy as he won't know what hit him.

And we are not only within the power of God, our loins are generating power. We are able to remain in the fight till the end, with our spiritual bowels still flowing when the battle is over. The reason this is so is because when we praying from our loins, even as we are giving out, we are reproducing power. We are also regenerating power.

Webster's Online Dictionary defines *Generative* as: having the power or function of generating, originating, producing, or reproducing

Therefore generative in and of itself is a continual process. It is never ending and free flowing. It is constantly producing, reproducing, replenishing as we pray. Instead of ending in weariness, we end with a release of freedom in our spirit. A release that doesn't drain, but yields a knowing that the ground and territory we just accomplished in the spirit realm will produce eternal natural fruit and harvest in our lives and sphere of influence. I encourage you to practice praying from your loins daily. You will see an entire dimensional shift in your ability to stand for God. Moreover, your spiritual discernment, stamina, hunger, drive, power, and authority in God will leap bounds daily and will set you apart as an atmosphere changer that is effective in producing the results of God and His kingdom.

THE BATTERING RAM

God desires to bring us to a place of fullness, particularly in this season of the body of Christ. In order to see fullness their will need to be a battering ram of some things.

Wikipedia Online Encyclopedia defines a *Battering Ram* as:

> *A battering ram is a siege engine originating in ancient times and designed to break open the masonry walls of fortifications or splinter their wooden gates. It was used, too, in ancient Roman mines and quarries to attack hard rocks. In its simplest form, a battering ram is just a large, heavy log carried by several people and propelled with force against an obstacle. The ram would be sufficient to damage the target if the log was massive enough and/or it were moved quickly enough, that is, if it had enough momentum.*

The church of God continues to wonder when the contending for the manifestations of God will end. But because God is progressive and constantly shifting and maneuvering, there will always be the need for contending. If you are a forerunner, then you have been ordained to be on the frontlines in some areas to set the standard and to open gateways for others to follow. As a forerunner you will have to contend and batter as this is part of the foundation of being able to shift, transform, and establish God's will and desires in your midst.

Ezekiel 4:2

(KJV)

And put siege works against it, build a siege wall against it, and cast up a mound against it; set camps also against it and set battering rams against it round about.

Ezekiel 21:22

(KJV)

In his right hand is the lot marked for Jerusalem: to set battering rams, to open the mouth calling for slaughter, to lift up the voice with a war cry, to set battering rams against the gates, to cast up siege mounds, and to build siege towers.

Batter in Merriam Webster's Online Dictionary means:

1. to beat persistently or hard; pound repeatedly

2. to damage by beating or hard usage

3. to deal heavy, repeated blows; pound steadily

4. any of various devices for battering, crushing, driving, or forcing something, esp. a battering ram

5. a heavy beak or spur projecting from the bow of a warship for penetrating the hull of an enemy's ship

6. a warship so equipped, esp. one used primarily for ramming enemy vessels.

7. the heavy weight that strikes the blow in a pile driver or the like.

8. to strike with great force; dash violently against

9. to cram; stuff, to push firmly

10. to force (a charge) into a firearm, as with a
    ramrod

As God shifts us to a greater dimension of
knowing Him and His will, emotions and
circumstance can't dictate our momentum and
alignment with His kingdom. It is important that
we move with him despite how we feel or what we
see as it is through this that we will be able to
experience His love and comfort of knowing He is
journeying with us and He is working. Therefore,
despite feelings and circumstances, our focus has
to be on what He has said and His will for our lives
and it is essential to have a drive to batter when the
enemy and the world is attempting to hinder us
from receiving what God has said or desires for us.

We worship through the knowing, we praise
through the knowing, we contend through the
knowing. And if there is something we aren't sure
of or God hasn't revealed yet, then we use the
weapon of a battering ram with what we want to
know and what we want to see come to pass.
There are new realms, new territories, new eras,
and even unfinished areas from previous years
that we must contend for so that fullness can come
or we continue to progress forward in the Lord. It
is our battering and our contending of those
manifestations that will bring them to pass.

As atmosphere changers, when situations occur in
our personal lives, it is essential to avoid becoming
self-focused as God has called us to a global work
therefore, we must purpose to have global eyes.

Strive to view through the bigger picture even though matters may seem personal, contending for the kingdom of God, affects family, church and the body of Christ as a whole. God will be about kingdom work and kingdom establishment in this new dimension of the kingdom. So even though the enemy will be about dividing and conquering with individual attacks, God will be focused on making heavens attributes our attributes and establishing the kingdom in every facet of our lives, ministries, and in our midst. He will be about kingdom and generational victories and establishing His kingdom among us. This doesn't mean God won't care about the things that happen to you personally. Yet as you fix your eyes on Him, He will take care of the matters of your heart, while you are caring for the matters of His heart.

Micah 2:13 discusses the spirit of the breaker, which essentially is what the battering ram does once he or she pushes to breakthrough.

> *(KJV)*
> *The breaker is come up before them: they have broken up, and have passed through the gate, and are gone out by it: and their king shall pass before them, and the LORD on the head of them.*
> *(Amplified)*
> *The [a]Breaker [the Messiah] will go up before them. They will break through, pass in through the gate and go out through it, and their King will pass on before them, the Lord at their head.*
>
> *(Message)*

*Then I, God, will burst all confinements and lead
them out into the open. They'll follow their
King. I will be out in front leading them."*

(NIV)
*I will open the way for you to return. I will
march in front of you. You will break through
the city gates and go free. I am your King. I will
pass through the gates in front of you. I will lead
the way.*

It is God that leads us as the battering ram. In this
passage of scripture, we see that He is called the
breaker, and is going ahead, to break through the
gates so that possession can take place.

<u>*Breaker* in the Hebrew is *Parats* and means:</u>
1. to break through or down or over, burst, breach
2. to break or burst out (from womb or enclosure)
3. to break through or down, make a breach in
4. to break into, to break open, break away
5. to break up, break in pieces
6. to break out (violently) upon
7. to break over (limits), increase
8. to use violence. to burst open

What God aspires us to break into is the fullness of
His kingdom being manifested in the earth.

Psalm 16:11
(KJV)
Thou wilt shew me the path of life: in thy presence is fulness of joy; at thy right hand there are pleasures for evermore.

Psalm 24:1
(KJV)
The earth is the LORD'S, and the fulness thereof; the world, and they that dwell therein.

Romans 15:29
(KJV)
And I am sure that, when I come unto you, I shall come in the fulness of the blessing of the gospel of Christ.

Ephesians 3:19
(KJV)
And to know the love of Christ, which passeth knowledge, that ye might be filled with all the fulness of God.

John 1:16
(KJV)
And of his fulness have all we received, and grace for grace.

Merriam Webster"s Online Dictionary defines of *fullness* as:

1. the quality or state of being full, in the fullness of time, at some point, eventually
2. completely filled; containing all that can be held; filled to utmost capacity

3. complete; entire; maximum, of the maximum size, amount, extent, volume, etc.

4. (of garments, drapery, etc.) wide, ample, or having ample folds

5. abundant; well-supplied, filled or rounded out

6. the highest or fullest state, condition, or degree

For so long many of us in the body of Christ have been walking in a measure of God. We have experienced minimal miracles, signs and wonders, and a measure of heaven in our households and lands. In this season, God is releasing some forerunners who will batter for fullness of His word and Kingdom in the earth realm; those that won't give into sin, weariness, worldliness, inconsistency, or settle for the mediocre.

As an atmosphere changer, you will know when you need to batter. You will know when you seem to have hit a wall or hindrance, and despite what God is saying, the circumstances or the spirit realm appears to be at a standstill in delivering the fruit and will of God. When this occurs, it is essential to stand contending for manifestation. The interesting thing about the weapon of a battering ram is that it has many forms and can be used in different ways. For example, you can batter with a song by singing or decreeing the same words over and over till you have pushed through. Our praise and worship team is excellent at battering with spiritual songs the Holy Spirit reveals, and as the words are sung over and over, you can hear and even see the enemy weakening and our church bursting through to victory.

You can batter with a movement the same way or batter with a scripture or prayer/decree. And sometimes you have to batter with your very life by just standing on what God is saying and decree it, and walk in it till God's word is revealed in your life and sphere of influence. Sometimes, it is generational walls and sins we are breaking through. Other times it is demonic fortresses that have been set up against us. And there are occasions when God will make us aware of a desire for our lives yet it is simply not the season for it, but the enemy will come after it in effort to abort it before it has a chance to manifest. Regardless of the reason, what God has said about you, your lineage, your church, your community, and nation is worth contending for. Don't settle for just enough when God has promised overflow. He has gone before you and is paving the way for your breakthrough.

Psalms 16:11

(KJV)
Thou wilt shew me the path of life: in thy presence [is] fulness of joy; at thy right hand [there are] pleasures for evermore.

BINDING & LOOSING

As atmosphere changers, binding and loosing is a very important weapon, as it is necessary to know our authority in being a key carrier of the kingdom and knowing how to use those keys to release heaven on earth.

Matthew 16:19

(KJV)
And I will give unto thee the keys of the kingdom of heaven: and whatsoever thou shalt bind on earth shall be bound in heaven: and whatsoever thou shalt loose on earth shall be loosed in heaven.

(NLT)
And I will give you the keys of the Kingdom of Heaven. Whatever you lock on earth will be locked in heaven, and whatever you open on earth will be opened in heaven."

(NIV)
And that's not all. You will have complete and free access to God's kingdom, keys to open any and every door: no more barriers between heaven and earth, earth and heaven. A yes on earth is yes in heaven. A no on earth is no in heaven.

(God's Word)
I will give you the keys of the kingdom of heaven. Whatever you imprison, God will imprison. And whatever you set free, God will set free.

(Amplified)

*I will give you the keys of the kingdom of heaven;
and whatever you bind (declare to be improper
and unlawful) on earth must be what is already
bound in heaven; and whatever you loose
(declare lawful) on earth must be what is already
loosed in heaven.*

Matthew 18:18

(KJV)

*Verily I say unto you, Whatsoever ye shall bind
on earth shall be bound in heaven: and
whatsoever ye shall loose on earth shall be loosed
in heaven. (Message)*

*Take this most seriously: A yes on earth is yes in
heaven; a no on earth is no in heaven. What you
say to one another is eternal. I mean this.*

(NLT)

*I tell you this: Whatever you prohibit on earth is
prohibited in heaven, and whatever you allow on
earth is allowed in heaven.*

(Amplified)

*Truly I tell you, whatever you forbid and declare
to be improper and unlawful on earth must be
what is already forbidden in heaven, and
whatever you permit and declare proper and
lawful on earth must be what is already
permitted in heaven.*

As you can see I love most of the Bible versions of
these two scriptures. All of them reveal a greater
detail of the power we have to bind and loose.
They also provide revelation that we have the

143

power to prohibit things that aren't from heaven
and allow access to those things that are.

The person with the key tends to have the power
and authority. That was my own personal
perception, yet when reviewing the definition of
keys in the Greek it reads as followed:

<u>Keys is *Kleis* and mean:</u>
1. a key
2. since the keeper of the keys has the power to
   open and to shut
3. In the NT to denote power and authority of
   various kinds

<u>Merriam Webster's Online Dictionary defines *Key*
as:</u>
1. a usually metal instrument by which the bolt of
   a lock is turned
2. any of various devices having the form or
   function of such a key
3. a means of gaining or preventing entrance,
   possession, or control
4. an instrumental or deciding factor
5. something that gives an explanation or
   identification or provides a solution

Binding and loosing is another way to control the
entrance ways. As the key holder, you are not
going to just let anyone in your personal home. As
the head of your household, you control who

comes in and who doesn't. And only under certain circumstances do you allow strangers to visit or dwell, and even then this encounter is brief and for purpose; and you definitely do not willingly cohabitate with strangers that are not for the good of your household, or that have evil and dangerous intents.

Therefore, just as with our natural houses so should it be with our spiritual houses, churches, neighborhoods, and sphere of influence.

When we consider a spiritual key, we have a threefold advantage occurring and that is:

> ➢ we ourselves are a key
> ➢ have been given the keys to access what we need from heaven
> ➢ if we don't know what key to use, we have access to the ultimate key holder.

The word says *"whatever we bind on earth is bound in heaven and whatever we loose on earth is loosed in heaven."*

<u>Bind</u> in the Greek is *Deo* and means:

1. to bind tie, fasten
2. to bind, fasten with chains, to throw into chains
3. Satan is said to bind a woman bent together by means of a demon, as his messenger, taking possession of the woman and preventing her from standing upright
4. to bind, put under obligation, of the law, duty etc.

145

5. to be bound to one, a wife, a husband

6. forbid, prohibit, declare to be illicit

Webster's Online Dictionary defines *Bind* as:

1. to make secure by tying, to confine, restrain, or restrict as if with bonds

2. to put under an obligation, to constrain with legal authority

3. to wrap around with something so as to enclose or cover, bandage

4. to fasten round about , to fasten or tie together

5. to cause to stick together, to take up and hold 6. to constipate

7. to protect, strengthen, or decorate by a band or binding

8. to apply the parts of the cover to

A key binds by stopping up the socket such that the enemy can no longer operate. As the definitions say, it essentially puts the enemy under obligation or the restraints of heaven. Just like it does when we put a key in a hole, our binding stops up or constipates the enemies" actions with the kingdom of heaven. When we are binding, we are essentially putting a vice grip on the enemy and his effect, while preventing him from working in our midst any longer. We are falling out of agreement with his ability to keep us bound and assert a greater power over his power.

Loose in the Greek is *Lyo* and means:

1. to loose any person (or thing) tied or fastened, bandages of the feet, the shoes,

2. to loose one bound, i.e. to unbind, release from bonds, set free

3. of one bound up (swathed in bandages)

4. bound with chains (a prisoner), discharge from prison, let go

5. to loosen, undo, dissolve, anything bound, tied, or compacted together

6. to an assembly, i.e. to dismiss, break up

7. to laws, as having a binding force, are likened to bonds, to annul, subvert

8. to do away with, to deprive of authority, whether by precept or act

9. to declare unlawful, to overthrow, to do away with

10. to loose what is compacted or built together, to break up, demolish, destroy

11. to dissolve something coherent into parts, to destroy

The Greek definition of loose is noteworthy because often when we consider loosing, we tend to release something in the place of that which we bind. For example, "I bind sickness and loose healing." And though that it also one of the ways to use our authority of loosing, the definitions of loosing also indicates being loosed from something that binds us, "*to loose any person or thing tied or*

fastened." Therefore, we can also loose ourselves
from things that would imprison or chain us. We
have the ability to loose ourselves from something
that has attached itself to us or our sphere of
influence in some way. For example, "I loose
myself from depression in Jesus name."

In the same way, we can also bind the enemy to his
own evils, there are times I will loose myself from
something the enemy has sent to me, and then I
bind him to it. For example, "I loose myself from
fear in Jesus and bind the enemy to it seven times
stronger." This is great during instances when one
is striving to bind and cast out something and it
will not go. Loosing essentially gives us the ability
to fall out of agreement with something such that
as it detaches or releases something that we desire
to take up residence with. It is important to make
sure you are loosing as much if not more than you
are binding, as loosing is a "releasing" of attributes
and the more we fill people and the earth with the
blessings of the kingdom, the less ground and
space the enemy can take up or regain.

Matthew 12:43-45

(KJV)

*When the unclean spirit is gone out of a man, he
walketh through dry places, seeking rest, and
findeth none. Then he saith, I will return into
my house from whence I came out; and when he
is come, he findeth [it] empty, swept, and
garnished. Then goeth he, and taketh with
himself seven other spirits more wicked than
himself, and they enter in and dwell there: and*

the last [state] of that man is worse than the first. Even so shall it be also unto this wicked generation.

When transforming atmospheres in people and climates, we have the keys to bind things that hinder heaven from being in our midst and we have the ability to loose the necessary attributes to manifest God's kingdom.

Luke 10:19 says:

(KJV)
Behold, I give unto you power to tread on serpents and scorpions, and over all the power of the enemy: and nothing shall by any means hurt you.

Verse 19-20 (Message)
See what I've given you? Safe passage as you walk on snakes and scorpions, and protection from every assault of the Enemy. No one can put a hand on you. All the same, the great triumph is not in your authority over evil, but in God's authority over you and presence with you. Not what you do for God but what God does for you – that's the agenda for rejoicing.
(Amplified)
Behold! I have given you authority and power to trample upon serpents and scorpions, and [physical and mental strength and ability] over all the power that the enemy [possesses]; and nothing shall in any way harm you.

Usually when the enemy has power over us, he has some legal ground or we haven't asserted proper authority or power over him. Often heaven hasn't come among us, because, we haven't asserted authority, and so we as a result we endure hardships that we really weren't to experience. The Amplified version of this scripture reveals to us that we have mental and physical strength and ability over all the power the enemy possesses. I have searched and searched this scripture, and sensed there has to be a complete knowing that we have been given such a triumphant authority in order to assert it. Yet many times, we tend to feel helpless or become weary which weakens the authority we have, and gives the enemy power over us. You see the enemy never stops trying to gain control and will take any avenue to gain a foothold. He is forever looking into the peephole of our lives, trying to see where he can come in and rob us. As a key holder, we have to know and walk in the authority as the gatekeeper, and remain open to the accountability and responsibility that comes with it; and that truly it is God who has given you this power and not you yourself. He really desires you to exercise it to its capacity so that the enemy's power can be snuffed out and His power in you can reign and govern your spiritual and natural homes and dwellings.

Binding and loosing is an effective way to strip the enemy of his legalities and his power, and to assert our dominion such that heaven can invade us. When there are closed heavens over churches, it is because they haven't asserted power. The enemy will take as much territory as we allow. It is up to us to use our keys to put him under our feet where

he belongs. Don't be afraid to bind and loose him
to the foot of Jesus where he belongs.

RELEASING THE REBUKES & STILLNESS OF THE LORD

Mark 4:36-41

(KJV)

And when they had sent away the multitude, they took him even as he was in the ship. And there were also with him other little ships. And there arose a great storm of wind, and the waves beat into the ship, so that it was now full. And he was in the hinder part of the ship, asleep on a pillow: and they awake him, and say unto him, Master, carest thou not that we perish? And he arose, and rebuked the wind, and said unto the sea, Peace, be still. And the wind ceased, and there was a great calm. And he said unto them, Why are ye so fearful? how is it that ye have no faith? And they feared exceedingly, and said one to another, What manner of man is this, that even the wind and the sea obey him?

The manner of man the disciples where experiencing in Mark 39 was King Jesus, the ultimate atmosphere changer. Storms, whether spiritually or natural are atmospheric in nature.

Storm in the Greek is *Laipops* and means:

1. a whirlwind, a tempestuous wind
2. a violent attack of wind, a squall
3. never a single gust nor a steady blowing wind, however violent, but a storm breaking forth from black thunder clouds in furious gusts,

with floods of rain, and throwing everything topsy-turvy

Storms are usually a violent assault or heavy influx of challenges that generally come with a sudden or unexpected onset. Storms usually cause much disturbance and create afflictions and even at times catastrophes. Just like the Bible story above, they are sent to instill fear, timidity and unbelief. They also cause such chaos and make so much noise, that our memory becomes void or blocked of the testimonies and miracles God has already done in our lives. And most often, we are so busy giving into the turbulence around us that forget we have power to rebuke the wind and command stillness to come to the roaring seas.

Jesus didn't take the disciples out of the storm or remove them from the situation. Instead, he used His power and authority to change the way the situation was impacting them. They were still in the water, still in the boat, still in the middle of the sea. The very thing that they thought was going to shake them to death, they road to shore, which was the storm. The storm didn't alter their course but when Jesus calmed the storm, they road it to the shore with ease.

When spiritual storms come against us, we are generally striving to get out of the situations. At times we have challenges confronting the storm and commanding it to submit to the power and presence of God that is in us. Rarely is our focus on using the storm, to coast us where God is
153

striving to take us. Generally we are yelling in fear and turmoil for God to deliver us out of the storm and God is shaking His head say, *"how is it that ye have no faith?"*

Jesus *rebuked* the wind (this is a key) and then said unto the sea, *peace* (another key), *be still* (another key). Three keys of weaponry:

> ➢ rebuke of the Lord
> ➢ declaring peace
> ➢ commanding stillness to the storm

Often we don't think of rebuking because it carries a negative connotation of being chastised or punished. It has been misused among the body of Christ, particularly when one is abusing their authority or using religious rules and scriptures in error. Yet the word says that if we are consistent tithe payers, He would rebuke the devourer on our behalf (Mal 3:11). So though rebuking may very be necessary in natural circumstances, it is an effective weapon that we can use to dispel the enemy.

Rebuke in the Greek is *Epitimaō*:

1. to show honour to, to honour
2. to raise the price of
3. to adjudge, award, in the sense of merited penalty
4. to tax with fault, rate, chide, rebuke, reprove, censure severely
5. to admonish or charge sharply

Jesus was sleeping comfortably when he was awakened by the terrified and appalled disciples who couldn't believe he had the audacity to sleep when their lives were at stake. The word says that Jesus then "rebuked the winds."

<u>*Wind* in the Greek is *Anemos*</u>
1. wind, a violent agitation and stream of air
2. a very strong tempestuous wind
3. the four principal or cardinal winds, hence the four corners of heaven

By rebuking the winds, Jesus thus commanded the tempestuous wind to show honor to Him and the disciples. I love the scripture that states how God's Spirit raises a standard when the enemy comes in like a flood (*Isaiah 59:19*). We will discuss the wind versus the flood in the next chapter, however, I do want to note, that we can discern from the Greek definition of rebuke that using this weapon gives way to God's Spirit manifesting and raising the standard around us to the original design and will He has for our lives. That Greek word "*Epitimao*" lets us know that God merits a penalty against the enemy, judges him, and fines him with a tax for bothering us. Therefore, when we loose the rebukes of the Lord against the enemy, we are judging what he is doing, declaring it unlawful, and releasing God's judgment and will in its place.

After Jesus rebuked the wind, He spoke "*peace*" to the raging seas.

155

<u>*Peace* in the Greek is *Sipao*:</u>

1. to be silent, hold one's peace
2. used of one's silence because dumb
3. of a calm, quiet sea

<u>*Peace* in Merriam Webster's Online dictionary
means:</u>

1. a state of tranquility or quiet, a freedom from
    civil disturbance
2. a state of security or order within a community
    provided for by law or custom
3. freedom from disquieting or oppressive
    thoughts or emotions harmony in personal
    relations
4. a state or period of mutual concord between
    governments
5. a pact or agreement to end hostilities between
    those who have been at war or in a state of
    enmity
    used interjectionally to ask for silence or calm
    or as a greeting or farewell
6. in a state of concord or tranquility, in a state
    without war
7. accord, amity, concord, harmony; calm, quiet,
    serenity, tranquility; order, stability;
    pacification

One thing we know about the sea is that it is full of
danger. To this day, explorers are still finding new
creatures and plants and the like in the sea. So

with all that is within a sea, we may know what is coming against us, and then there are situations, where we don't have a clue, what is raging war against us. But Jesus has proved to us that peace can silence the sea.

From the Merriam Webster's dictionary, we would think that Jesus made a treaty or agreement with the seas when He spoke peace, however,

The Primitive Root Word for *Peace* in the Greek is *Sige* and means:
1. to silence
2. hush
3. yield proper muteness
4. bring involuntary stillness
5. inability to speak

Just like Jesus, we should never make any agreements with the devil, even at the sake of experiencing some relief. Yet we should assert our God given authority and tell the devil to be silent, to hush; to basically shut up as Jesus did when He spoke peace to the sea.

After Jesus told the sea to hush by speaking, "*Peace*," He told it to "*Be Still.*" We would think that once Jesus told the sea to hush, it would have automatically calmed and stop raging. I sense that Jesus said, "*Peace*" to deal with the noise that was coming from the turbulence of the sea and then said "*Be Still* "so everything that was causing the

157

noise could not only hush, but stop moving and affecting them. It appears that the sea was at an all out war, so it was making all kinds of racket and then tossing them to and fro, which just increased the fear and panic of the disciples.

Be Still in the Greek _is Phimoō_ and means:

1. to close the mouth with a muzzle, to muzzle
2. to stop the mouth, make speechless, reduce to silence
3. to become speechless
4. to be kept in check

When Jesus said "Be Still," He was closing the mouth of the enemy by putting a muzzle over it.

Muzzle in Merriam Webster's Online Dictionary is defined as:

1. the projecting jaws and nose of an animal, snout
2. a fastening or covering for the mouth of an animal used to prevent eating or biting
3. something (as censorship) that restrains normal expression the open end of an implement; _especially_ : the discharging end of a weapon

Some of the Thesaurus words for *muzzle* are as followed:

gag	crack down	prevent quiet repress
quiet	on curb	restrain restrict shush
bottle	dry up dummy	shut down silence
up	up	
censor	hush, ice	
check	muffle	
choke		
clamp		
down		
on		
cork		

WHEW!!!! Gag that enemy! Stop glorying Taquetta! WHEWWW!!!

We can discern from Jesus, that we can't bind a storm. We can't cast a storm out. But when Jesus used His weapons of *rebuke, peace, and stillness*, the storm dissipated into the air as if it was never there. His weaponry evaporated or even was swallowed up with the weapons He used. Jesus silenced and muzzled the storm. The silence is what quieted and declared the war was over, but it could have still kept going even though it was quiet, so Jesus in turn, muzzled it. He gagged it. The muzzling and gagging prevented the sea from continuing to tear through things while the silencing stopped the chaos and noise and the declaration of war that it was making. We don't even know if the storm on the whole sea went

159

away but for the place where they were, calmness came via these weapons.

The wind is atmospheric in that it affects the environment, the air, and that which is in the heavenlies. The wind therefore, touches and impacts anything that is exposed to it. The sea is territorial as it encompasses a body of water and covers a vast of land. A sea entails water which we need for survival and denotes mobility as waters tend move and cover. We are to possess dominion over the winds (air) and the sea (movement).

Genesis 1:28
(KJV)
And God blessed them, and God said unto them, Be fruitful, and multiply, and replenish the earth, and subdue it: and have dominion over the fish of the sea, and over the fowl of the air, and over every living thing that moveth upon the earth.

God ordained us when He first made creation to have dominion over the wind and the sea. He ordained us to control the airways and the land. It is essential that when demonic powers wage war, and send storms into our lives, churches, and sphere of influence, that we stand in a place of dominion and rebuke, silence and muzzle these storms. We have the power to shift the atmosphere to tranquility and manifest the attributes of heaven such that we ride the very thing that was raging against us to victory.

THE FLOOD VERSUS THE WIND

Isaiah 59:19

> *(KJV)*
>
> *So shall they fear the name of the LORD from the west, and his glory from the rising of the sun. When the enemy shall come in like a flood, the Spirit of the LORD shall lift up a standard against him.*

Merriam Webster's Online Dictionary defines *Flood* as:

1. a great flowing or overflowing of water, especially over land not usually submerged

2. any great outpouring or stream

3. the rise or flowing in of the tide

4. Archaic. a large body of water.

5. to overflow in or cover with a flood

6. to cover or fill, as if with a flood

7. to overwhelm with an abundance of something: to be flooded with mail

8. to flow or pour in or as if in a flood

9. to rise in a flood; overflow

So the devil comes in with His flood, interesting. If you have never been in a flood, let me tell you from experience that it can be a bit overwhelming. When I was about nine years old, my family and I were returning to our home in East Saint, Louis, Illinois after visiting family in Mississippi. East Saint Louis, Illinois is divided from Saint Louis

Missouri by the Mississippi River. And one summer, due to heavy rain, the floodgates broke and the Mississippi river flooded our city.

When we first entered the city, the water wasn't that high and some streets weren't flooded yet. We maneuvered our way around to our home and not really knowing what was going on at the time, we drove the cars up in the yard and sloshed our way into the house. By the next day however, the flood waters had covered our cars and porches, and was making its" way into the house. Rescuers on boats had to come get us out of the homes and take us to safety.

After the water was cleared and we returned to our homes, much of our things were damaged beyond repair and we had to replace most things. Everything was wet, stunk and covered in debris and filth from the flood. Not to mention the Mississippi waters themselves were contaminated due to every kind of disgusting thing being in the waters so it wasn't even realistic to clean everything and feel contentment that it was sanitized properly.

Worms and all kinds of dead and squirming animals were everywhere and truly I had nightmares for months trying to get over creepy crawlies and the experience in general. I remember being sent to a friend's house when it was time to go clean the house as my mom felt it just wasn't worth the trauma I was exhibiting from seeing the damage and effects of everything. It can be quite a traumatic and painful event and unlike us, others where physically hurt, some drowned; and it took years for many families to recover naturally and spiritually from the experience.

The attributes that occur in a natural flood are similar to those that occur when the enemy comes into our lives, flooding us with havoc and turmoil, however, the enemy's flood is even more damaging. Yet unlike the floodgates in the natural that have the tendency to break, the floodgates of God's wind are secure and have the power to hold back and/or dry up any flood of the enemy such that it would appear that it never manifested in our lives.

Isaiah contends that *"When the enemy shall come in like a flood, the Spirit of the LORD shall lift up a standard against him."* God is alerting us in this scripture that when the enemy attacks us like a flood, there is a standard that counterattacks and literally lifts this flood off of us, from around us, and from our sphere of influence.

The spirit of the Lord lifts up a standard by violently judging that flood.

Standard in the Hebrew is *Nuwc* and means:
1. to flee
2. to escape
3. to take flight, depart, disappear
4. to fly (to the attack) on horseback

163

5. to drive at

6. to take flight

7. to put to flight

8. to drive hastily

9. to cause to disappear, hide

God's standard manifests in the form of His Spirit and sends that flood fleeing in terror, while causing it to disappear as if it never formed. When God's spirit enters your midst, that flood is literally looking for a way of escape. It knows that it has been judged and defeated and even as God is driving it out, it is running hastily from the wrath of God. This is because when God's Spirit manifests, it comes in as a death blowing wind. As a refresher from the an earlier chapter where we discussed God's Spirit,

Spirit in Isaiah 49:19 is *Ruwach* and is defined as:

1. wind, breath, mind, spirit,

2. quarter (of wind), side, breath of air, air, gas

3. spirit, animation, vivacity, vigour, courage,

4. temper, anger, impatience, patience

5. of heaven, breath of air, heaven

6. spirit (as that which breathes quickly in animation or agitation)

7. spirit, animation, vivacity, vigour, courage

8. prophetic spirit, as inspiring ecstatic state of prophecy

9. as gift, preserved by God, God's spirit, departing at death, disembodied being

10. spirit (as seat of emotion), desire, as seat or organ of mental acts,

11. rarely of the will, as seat especially of moral character

12. Spirit of God, the third person of the triune God, the Holy Spirit, coequal, coeternal with the Father and the Son

13. imparting warlike energy and executive and administrative power

14. as endowing men with various gifts, as energy of life

15. as manifest in the Shekinah glory

The Message Version of Isaiah 49:19 reads:

In the west they'll fear the name of God, in the east they'll fear the glory of God, For he'll (the devil) arrive like a river in flood stage, whipped to a torrent by the wind of God.

The *Ruwach* winds of God drives out the flood of Satan! How does this happen? It happens because the wind of God whips that flood to a torrent.

Merriam Webster's Online Definition of torrent is:

1. a stream of water flowing with great rapidity and violence

2. a rushing, violent, or abundant and unceasing stream of anything, a torrent of lava

3. a violent downpour of rain

4. a violent, tumultuous, or overwhelming flow, a torrent of abuse

5. a tumultuous outpouring , rush

6. a violent stream of a liquid (as water or lava)

7. a channel of a mountain stream

Merriam Webster's Online Definition of whipped is:

1. having received a whipping.

2. subdued or defeated as though by whipping: whipped by poverty

3. beaten into a froth: whipped cream

4. exhausted, tired, beat: Beat with a pistol

Whip in Merriam Webster's Online Dictionary means:

1. to beat with a strap, lash, rod, or the like, especially by way of punishment or chastisement; flog;

2. to strike with quick, repeated strokes of something slender and flexible; lash

3. to drive with lashes; urge or force on with, or as with, a lash, rod, etc.

4. to lash or castigate with words, to unite, bring together, or bring into line

5. to defeat or overcome: to whip the opposition; to whip a bad habit.

6. to hoist or haul by means of a whip.

166

7. to move quickly and suddenly; pull, jerk, seize, or the like, with a sudden

8. to wind (cord, twine, thread, etc.) about something:

9. to move or go quickly and suddenly; dart; whisk

10. to beat or lash about, as a pennant in the wind, punish

The Amplified Bible of Isaiah 49:19 reads:

> *So [as the result of the Messiah's intervention] they shall [reverently] fear the name of the Lord from the west, and His glory from the rising of the sun. When the enemy shall come in like a flood, the Spirit of the Lord will lift up a standard against him and put him to flight [for He will come like a rushing stream which the breath of the Lord drives].*

The Spirit of the Lord delivers us from the flood, by releasing a wind that strikes the enemy so violently, it drives Him from our midst. In *Exodus 10:13*, we see God using Moses to bring forth a wind of judgment when Pharaoh refused to let the His people go.

> *And Moses stretched forth his rod over the land of Egypt, and the LORD brought an east wind upon the land all that day, and all [that] night; [and] when it was morning, the east wind brought the locusts.*

God had Ezekiel prophecy to the wind and tell it to breathe, blow upon a dead army and restore life.

The wind was judging death and reviving it with the breath of heaven.

Ezekiel 37:9

(KJV)

Then said he unto me, Prophesy unto the wind, prophesy, son of man, and say to the wind, Thus saith the Lord GOD; Come from the four winds, O breath, and breathe upon these slain, that they may live.

There are many accounts throughout the Bible where God sent the wind of His Spirit or led others to use His wind to judge the attacks of the enemy. Often during praise and worship, we feel the winds of God's Spirit blowing and we enjoy them, which is great, but rarely do we consider utilizing His presence to drive out darkness and spiritual floods that are occurring among us. At times, God will go ahead and drive out the enemy; nonetheless, there are other times, when He desires us to utilize His presence to whip the enemy. He wants us to prophesy to the winds and declare His judgment in our midst. God wants us to be aware that He is pistol whipping the enemy on our behalf and that we have access to His presence to defeat and send the enemy running in terror. I strongly encourage you to conduct a personal Bible study the word *"wind"* and the *"Spirit of the Lord"* and seek God for greater revelation on this great weaponry lifting up a standard for you against floods that occur in your life, church, and atmosphere.

DEFUSING THE ENEMY

There are times the Lord will reveal spiritual weaponry to me, depending on what I am experiencing, or the assignments He has granted to my hands, or to those around me. There are also instances when I am ministering and I am not sure what God is having me combat in the spirit realm, but I am aware that He is using me to dismantle a demonic power structure and bring forth His will and desires for those people, that ministry, or in that sphere into fruition.

One particular Sunday someone took an interesting picture of me that looked like my hands had entered the spirit realm while I was ministering in dance during praise and worship and was squeezing the head of a demon. As I was squeezing it, it appeared to be getting smaller. I inquired with God about the picture, and He said I was *"defusing the enemy."*

Defuse in Merriam Webster's Online Dictionary means:

1. to remove the fuse/fuze from (a bomb, mine, etc.).
2. to make less dangerous, potent, tense, or embarrassing
3. to defuse a potentially ugly situation.
4. to grow less dangerous; weaken, defuse

The Thesaurus synonyms of *Defuse* are:
alleviate, diminish pacify cripple disable restrain deactivate lesson soften demilitarize modify soothe

During that service, we were having a difficult time remaining inside the presence of the Lord and thus began to declare our authority over enemy so that he would totally be disposed. And the dancers begin to minister warfare movements against the enemy such that when the picture was taken, it captured the Lord using us to subdue dominion over the enemy.

God made it clear from His first blessing of man that we are to walk in dominion, and to subdue of the earth. Yet I know I personally tend to have challenges in knowing just how to do this so that dominion reins every place the souls of my feet tread.

Genesis 1:28 states:
> *(KJV)*
> *And God blessed them, and God said unto them, Be fruitful, and multiply, and replenish the earth, and subdue it: and have dominion over the fish of the sea, and over the fowl of the air, and over every living thing that moveth upon the earth.*

Subdue in the Hebrew is *Kabash* and means:

1. to subject, subdue, force, keep under, bring into bondage
2. to bring into bondage, make subservient
3. to subdue, force, violate
4. to subdue, dominate, tread down

170

When we defuse the enemy, we are subduing him and making him subject to the presence of God in us and around us. We are disconnecting and severing the enemy's connections from the power sources that are coming from the second heavens (principalities), such that it can no longer have authority over us and our surroundings. God has given us the authority to squeeze the headships of demonic kingdoms, such that it subjects them to His bondage and gives us access to tread upon them and take over their land. One great fact about subduing is that as long as you are in right standing with the Lord, it keeps the enemy under your feet. It isn't territory that you have to conquer again for it is an inheritance that was given to us and thus is an eternal reward from the Lord.

Psalms 47:2-4

(KJV)

For the LORD most high [is] terrible; [he is] a great King over all the earth. He shall subdue the people under us, and the nations under our feet. He shall choose our inheritance for us, the excellency of Jacob whom he loved. Selah.

The weapon of defusing is used when it appears the enemy is triumphing over you, a situation, or a sphere and he needs to be subjected to the servitude of the Lord.

Exodus 8:13

(KJV)

Then came Amalek, and fought with Israel in Rephidim. And Moses said unto Joshua, Choose us out men, and go out, fight with Amalek: tomorrow I will stand on the top of the hill with the rod of God in mine hand. So Joshua did as Moses had said to him, and fought with Amalek: and Moses, Aaron, and Hur went up to the top of the hill. And it came to pass, when Moses held up his hand, that Israel prevailed: and when he let down his hand, Amalek prevailed.

But Moses' hands [were] heavy; and they took a stone, and put [it] under him, and he sat thereon; and Aaron and Hur stayed up his hands, the one on the one side, and the other on the other side; and his hands were steady until the going down of the sun. And Joshua discomfited Amalek and his people with the edge of the sword.

Discomfited in the Hebrew is *Chalash* and means:

1. to be weak, be prostrate
2. to weaken, disable, prostrate

As long as Moses hands were up, Joshua and his army would be winning the battle. When Moses arms tired, and they started to fall, they would start to loose. But Aaron and Hur stood by Moses and help up His hands. Moses hands remaining in a posture of praise and victory unto God, discomfited, defused, weakened, disable, the power of the enemy and laid Amalek and his people prostrate in defeat at the feet of Joshua and the Israelites.

As atmosphere changers, God will give you different strategies to use the weapon of defusing. When He does, no matter how strange it seems, be obedient as He simply is giving you victory to disengage the power source and structure of the enemy.

DISMANTLING PRINCIPALITIES

One night the Lord gave me a dream about dismantling principalities using the sevenfold anointing of the Holy Spirit. In my dream a few youngsters and I, were playing basketball, though there wasn't the use of a ball or the presence of a goal. I was showing them full court defensive strategies against the enemy. We were playing full court three on three scrimmages, and the objective appeared to be to get around your enemy.

One of the youngsters came on the court and she was paired with her opponent. As I begin to show her a few strategies she took off and outsmarted her opponent. Once she made it pass the enemy, her head performed a tick motion seven times in seven different directions, but from one side to the other. It was as if her head was a camera and she was taking pictures of her enemy. I could literally hear the flashes as she ticked but her head was not taking literal pictures, it was dismantling the enemy as that is what the Holy Spirit said to me as I watched her in action. Only her head moved and she wasn't displaying this against her opponent, but a literal enemy in the spirit realm and myself and the others could literally hear his defeat as she her head performed the ticking motion.

There were several scriptures the Lord led to me concerning this dream.

Deuteronomy 28:7

> *(KJV)*
> *The Lord shall cause thine enemies that rise up against thee to be smitten before thy face: they shall come out against thee one way, and flee before thee seven ways.*

Isaiah 11:2

> *(KJV)*
> *And the spirit of the LORD shall rest upon him, the spirit of wisdom and understanding, the spirit of counsel and might, the spirit of knowledge and of the fear of the LORD;*

I searched this dream further with some interpreter friends of mines, and we all sensed the head ticking represented the authority and ruler-ship of the sevenfold manifestation of the Holy Spirit we see listed in *Isaiah 11:2*. Being able to dismantle not just your enemy but a principality and see him flee seven ways is, at times, contingent upon the blessings of *Deuteronomy 28* flowing in your life. And to see such manifestations, one must pursue the fullness of the Spirit of the Lord operating in your life.

In the dream we were on the defense as I was teaching defensive strategies.

Merriam Webster's Online Dictionary defines *Defensive* as:

1. serving to defend or protect <defensive fortifications>

175

2. devoted to resisting or preventing aggression or attack <defensive behavior>
3. of or relating to the attempt to keep an opponent from scoring in a game or contest
4. valuable in defensive play
5. designed to keep an opponent from being the highest bidder

Our defensive strategies was good but the Lord revealed to me that the head ticking youngster's strategy was more offensive, that is why it had a greater and more effective impact that brought grand results.

Merriam Webster's Online Dictionary defines *Offensive* as:
1. making attack, aggressive, of, relating to, or designed for attack <offensive weapons>
2. of or relating to an attempt to score in a game or contest; also
3. of or relating to a team in possession of the ball or puck giving painful or unpleasant sensations, nauseous, obnoxious
4. causing displeasure or resentment

When on defense you are attempting to stop an opponent. On the offense, you are striving to score on an opponent.

Often when combating the enemy, we strive to be on the defensive and think more counter attack, rather than be offensive and focused on attacking the enemy before he attacks. I have heard all kinds of religious jargon about not stirring up the devil and not tempting the devil. The devils thinks about none of this when he is attacking us; and truly though we aren't to glory over the fact that we have power over the enemy, the word says nothing about us needing to wait till the enemy attacks us to attack him. Actually the word speaks of how this mindset has caused the kingdom to suffer great violence, and though we have taken it by force it has cost us great turmoil and hardship.

Matthew 11:12

(KJV)
And from the days of John the Baptist until now the kingdom of heaven suffereth violence, and the violent take it by force.

(Amplified)
And from the days of John the Baptist until the present time, the kingdom of heaven has endured violent assault, and violent men seize it by force [as a precious prize--a share in the heavenly kingdom is sought with most ardent (eager, fiery, hot, shinning, glowing) zeal and intense (extreme), exertion].

We assume that this scripture is telling us to be violent pursuers of the kingdom. And indeed it is, however, it is also expressing, that all the subduing that was done before John the Baptist, has caused great bloodshed and hardship. Though we are to be violent against the enemy, we are also to have great zeal and intense exertion to stand in the face of the enemy. That doesn't mean wait till the enemy starts beating us down to attack him. But because we know he attacks, we are to live a daily walk on the offensive eager to engage him, such that we are subduing the enemy before he can even consider his next move against us. We tend to bench those who have great zeal and fervor for the Lord. We see them as threats to exposing us to the enemy when really we should take them under our wings, teach them a bit of wisdom, and let them launch on out in the deep and subdue the kingdom for the Lord.

It is the sevenfold anointing of the Holy Spirit that was dismantling the principality and causing him to flee seven ways and it was done by attacking the enemy before it had a chance to attack. The sevenfold anointing is a display of attributes where one is submitted to the presence, wisdom, counsel, understanding, might, and fear of the Lord. They are not walking in their own authority and counsel, but are fully submitted to the voice and will of God for their lives and destinies. They do what Jesus says and only what He says and follow His heart concerning all their endeavors. Under such a mantle, one doesn't have to fear being overtaken by the enemy or wait for the enemy to attack to counter attack. With such a submission, one can offensively journey in and declare the collapsing of the enemy's camp and see God's Kingdom take its possession.

In my dream we were on a full court. The week before I had a similar dream and it was half court.

Half court I believe represents the church and full court represents the kingdom. Therefore, our mindsets for defeating the enemy has to be not just in relations to the church and gaining territory within our body, but having a pursuit of the earth for the betterment of the kingdom of God as a whole. We have to have a kingdom mindset in our agenda to defeat the enemy in this hour, and we must possess the sevenfold spirit of God so we can offensively dismantle principalities and release God's dominion in their place.

DIVINE FORCE FIELD

In June of 2010, I kept having a vision of where I was seeing myself inside the protected barrier/bubble that looks like a protective wire fence. Yet the fence didn't look real, but more like a radiating fence surrounding me. I continued to hear the Holy Spirit say, "force field" so of course I explored the definition of the word.

I found out through Wikipedia, that a *Force Field*,
> *"Sometimes known as an energy shield, force shield, or deflector shield is a barrier, typically made of energy or charged particles that protects a person, area or object from attacks or intrusions. Force fields tend to appear often in works of speculative fiction."*

Merriam Webster's Online Dictionary defines a *Force Field* as:
1. a field
2. a special charm, aura, or spirit that can influence anyone in its presence
3. something resembling a force field especially in intensity that restricts or impedes movement toward an area or object

The Lord said that I was to use the force field to create a glory dome. I didn't know what the Lord was talking about so asked my mentor who further explained that sometimes the Lord will use His glory over a place as a force field, so that it exerts his glory rather than the enemy's demonic rays. The Lord then expressed further to me that He His glory would be like a dome that seals the enemy's power with a protective shield so that it can no long move or affect anything around it. And that the glory itself would then take possession of that thing or sphere and radiates His power and authority such that it transforms the environment and the people for His glory.

This was all new and very fascinating to me till I almost wanted to keep it to myself for fear that I would appear weird. Yet the Lord gave my church a particular assignment in the city and led me to share the vision with my leadership who were very receptive. He had us use the glory dome to quench the powers and effects of a major principality in our area, and since that time, we have seen continual and immediate upward shifts in our church, in the atmosphere, and in our town.

While writing this chapter, I asked the Lord exactly what a force field was in Biblical terms and He said a shield and led me to multiple scriptures.

Psalms 3:3
> *(KJV)*
> *But thou, O LORD, [art] a shield for me; my glory, and the lifter up of mine head.*

Psalms 18:35
> *(KJV)*

Thou hast also given me the shield of thy
salvation: and thy right hand hath holden me up,
and thy gentleness hath made me great.

Psalms 35:2
(KJV)
Take hold of shield and buckler, and stand up for
mine help.

Psalms 84:11
(KJV)
For the Lord God [is] a sun and shield: the Lord
will give grace and glory: no good [thing] will he
withhold from them that walk uprightly.

Psalms 119:114
(KJV)
Thou [art] my hiding place and my shield: I hope
in thy word.

The primitive root word for *Shield* in the Hebrew is
Ganan and means:
to defend, cover, surround

Merriam Webster's Online Dictionary defines
Shield as:

1. a broad piece of defensive armor carried on the arm
2. one that protects or defends, defends
3. dress shield
4. device or part that serves as a protective cover or barrier

5. a protective structure

Thesaurus synonyms for Shield are as followed:

ammunition	safeguard	arm
armor screen	armament buckler	security munitions
cover shield	weapon guard	wall weaponry
protection	ward	fastness

Basically He uses His glory to shield us from the enemy. He does a twofold work, because He secures the enemy's grip tightly inside His glory while also radiating His glory to us so that we get the effect of His presence that is shielding us from the enemy. When we usually think of shield we just think of something that protects us from spears and the like and usually we have to be very aware in knowing where the spear is coming from, otherwise if we don't get the shield up in time or have it in the proper position, we risk being hit by the enemy. But God's shield surrounds and covers us. It is a stronghold that encompasses us and fastens us inside His presence, His divine force field.

<u>The Message version of Psalms 3:3 reads:</u>
> *But you, GOD, shield me on all sides; You ground my feet, you lift my head high;*

It is noteworthy that David, the most premiere worshipper, speaks a lot of God shielding him. We would assume this was because of all the wars he had to combat and it is very much a true assessment. But I believe David understood that without the presence of God, he would have died in war. He understood that it was the glorious presence of the Lord that truly protected him from His enemies, demolished their plans against him and enable Him to be victorious in His reign as King. We see this in *Psalms 91* as David speaks about dwelling in the secret place, the divine force field of the Most High God.

Psalms 91:1-4

(KJV)

He that dwelleth in the secret place of the most High shall abide under the shadow of the Almighty. I will say of the LORD, He is my refuge and my fortress: my God; in him will I trust. Surely he shall deliver thee from the snare of the fowler, and from the noisome pestilence. He shall cover thee with his feathers, and under his wings shalt thou trust: his truth shall be thy shield and buckler.

(Amplified)

He who dwells in the secret place of the Most High shall remain stable and fixed under the shadow of the Almighty [Whose power no foe can withstand]. I will say of the Lord, He is my Refuge and my Fortress, my God; on Him I lean and rely, and in Him I [confidently] trust! For [then] He will deliver you from the snare of the fowler and from the deadly pestilence. [Then] He will cover you with His pinions, and under

His wings shall you trust and find refuge; His truth and His faithfulness are a shield and a buckler.

(Message)
You who sit down in the High God's presence, spend the night in Shaddai's shadow, Say this: "GOD, you're my refuge. I trust in you and I'm safe!" That's right – he rescues you from hidden traps, shields you from deadly hazards. His huge outstretched arms protect you – under them you're perfectly safe; his arms fend off all harm.

David knew the safety of the glory dome of God. And he knew how it isolated and defended the enemy. As you read further in *Psalms 91*, David clearly identifies what enemies are being defeated and how no terrors of the night or destructions of the noonday can touch him as he is sheltered inside the presence of the Lord.

There are times, the Lord will have me release a divine force field over my home to protect and shield my home and assets from the plows of the enemy. I have also used the force field in ministry to isolate a congregation from the influences of the enemy so that they can receive what God is saying and be transformed in His presence. I believe that what David was describing in *Psalms 91* was the workings of a principality that was constantly wreaking havoc among him and his kingdom. When you are continually being influenced by a principality that has taken over our cities, states, and nations, ask God to lead you in where to place

His divine force field, such that the works of the enemy can be hindered, and His judgment and kingdom can be established in its place.

In conclusion, this book is only a mere glimpse of the weapons God has to conquer the enemy. I pray it stirred your Spirit to pursue Him for even more weaponry and strategies to defeat the enemy, shift and transform atmospheres, and manifest the kingdom of Heaven in the earth realm. Don't limit God and He won't limit you. You are the first weapon and He will only add to your collection, while equipping you to be a weapon of mass destruction for His glory.

Resources & Scripture References:

- ❖ Biblegateway.com
- ❖ Blueletterbible.com
- ❖ Crosswalk.com
- ❖ *Dance and Fivefold Ministry* by Taquetta Baker
- ❖ Merriam-Webster.com
- ❖ *Scripture Look At Dance*, Apostle Pamela Hardy
- ❖ *Worship In Dance* by Richard A. Murphy, 1998
- ❖ *Prophetic Dance*, By Apostle Pamela Hardy
- ❖ Wikipedia.com

Taquetta's Contact Info:

(Website) Kingdomshifters.com
Connect with Taquetta via Facebook & Youtube

Cover Design and Layout:

Book Picture Cover is by Tashema Davis and layout design by Reenita Keys
Connect with them via Facebook

Made in the USA
Coppell, TX
18 December 2023

25576170R10108